THE
ARIZONA
DIVORCE
HANDBOOK

YOUR STEP BY STEP GUIDE
TO NAVIGATE ARIZONA DIVORCE

THE
ARIZONA
DIVORCE
HANDBOOK

YOUR STEP BY STEP GUIDE
TO NAVIGATE ARIZONA DIVORCE

Scott David Stewart, Esq.

An Imprint of Stewart Law Group

www.ArizonaLawGroup.com

SDS Legal Marketing LLC USA, Publisher
777 E Thomas Rd Ste 150, Phoenix AZ 85014
sdslegalmarketing.com

SECOND EDITION
ISBN 978-0-9886052-9-9

For information please write the publisher:

SDS Legal Marketing LLC
777 E Thomas Rd Ste 150
Phoenix AZ 85014

Legal Disclaimer

The general information in this book is not, nor is it intended to be, specific legal advice. You should consult an attorney for specific legal advice regarding your individual situation and circumstances.

This book is provided as a general reference work and is for informational purposes only. You are advised to check for changes to current law and to consult with a qualified attorney on any legal issue. The receipt of or use of this book does not create an attorney-client relationship with Stewart Law Group, its principals, or any of its attorneys.

Because this book was prepared for general readership without investigation into the facts of each particular case, it is not legal advice. Neither Stewart Law Group nor any of its attorneys has an attorney-client relationship with you. The thoughts and commentary about the law contained in this book are provided merely as a public service and do not constitute solicitation or legal advice.

While we endeavored to provide accurate information in this book, we cannot guarantee that the material provided herein is accurate, adequate, or complete. This general legal information is provided on an 'as is' basis. We make no warranties and disclaim liability for damages resulting from its use. Legal advice must be tailored to the specific circumstances of each case and laws are constantly changing. Therefore, nothing provided in this book should be used as a substitute for the advice of competent legal counsel.

The material in this book may be considered advertising under applicable rules.

Contents

Dedication

Dedicated to those families struggling through transition, looking for help and guidance, while focusing on the needs, hopes, and dreams of their children.

Acknowledgements

My thanks to the family law team at the firm who so generously shared their ideas for revising this second edition of The Arizona Divorce Handbook. To Laura Valade, JD, whose creative input and editing helped translate my vision for the book into reality. And to my amazing family who unfailingly embrace my every new project with infectious enthusiasm and loving support.

Author's Note

I originally wrote the *The Arizona Divorce Handbook: Your Step By Step Guide to Navigate Arizona Divorce* as a guide for individuals contemplating the possibilities of divorce and to be a valuable resource for someone already engaged in a pending divorce action. I'm pleased to say those same goals remain the focus of this second edition of the handbook.

I stress throughout my book how getting a divorce education is essential to achieving the best possible outcome in your case. In divorce, knowledge is power!

Reading through these chapters, you will quickly gain insight into the main issues in divorce, enabling you to make truly informed decisions. The choices you make during the divorce process will have long-lasting consequences for you, for the other party, and for your children. Preparing for your new life after the divorce decree is entered necessarily requires advance study and planning for each phase of the dissolution process.

There are legal procedures beyond the scope of this book which I wrote as a useful overview of basic Arizona divorce issues. You are sure to have specific questions particular to your family's circumstances and legitimate concerns about what happens after the divorce should something change regarding the children, such as a parent's relocation, request for increased or decreased child support, or petition to modify the parenting plan.

As you read each chapter, freely visit my law firm's website at www.ArizonaLawGroup.com and utilize it as a supplementary resource to your studies. You will find an extensive library on divorce proceedings and ADR, property division, legal decision-making and parenting time, grandparent and third-party visitation, child support and spousal maintenance, domestic violence and orders of protection, and more.

One quick note before you get started. Arizona law no longer uses the term "child custody," using instead the terms "legal decision-making" and "parenting time." Because it is still in common usage and recognized by most readers, I sometimes use "child custody" when referring to global issues in a general sense. In all other discussions, I specify "legal decision-making" and "parenting time" with particularity.

Scott David Stewart
Attorney at Law

INTRODUCTION
Navigating Arizona Divorce

Are you contemplating divorce, but have no clue where to begin? Did your spouse already serve you with a summons and court papers? Are you seriously concerned with protecting your spousal and parental rights? Do you know how legal decision-making and parenting time (previously called child custody) will be decided for your children? If you have questions like these, then this book is the ideal place to begin your Arizona divorce education.

To successfully launch your studies, the materials in this book are organized in such a way as to introduce you to each phase of the divorce process.

In **Chapter 1 – *Divorce: Making the Most Difficult Decision and Carrying It Out* –** I offer thoughtful information on how best to handle the emotional aspects of divorce, which is no small task. This important discussion is intended to help you avoid being overwhelmed with the seriousness and number of decisions you must make. These are decisions that will impact your finances, your lifestyle, your happiness, and the future you hope to provide for your children.

I talk about voluntary participation in *marriage counseling* and *divorce counseling* because either or both may be very beneficial to you. Getting started on something this big is made easier with instructions, so I've provided a "To Do" list to help you begin planning and preparing for your divorce.

In this chapter you will also read about Arizona's traditional marriage and *covenant marriage*, the grounds for divorce necessary to dissolve each, and what to do from there. In my roadmap to divorce, I steer you through an overview of the court process required to dissolve the marriage. You'll get a bird's eye view of what to expect in your case. Whether you have minor children or not, Chapter 1 will give you much needed guidance and direction.

Chapter 2 — *Parenting Plans: Who Gets the Kids?* — covers the basic information you need to know regarding custody of your child. I discuss the requirements of a parenting plan along with what distinguishes *legal decision-making* authority from *parenting time* in Arizona law. I cover the professional facilitators who work with parents to help resolve custody conflicts — namely mediators, parenting coordinators, and child custody evaluators. I also include some very important child custody tips so you know what to do and what not to do when under custody orders.

If you have a minor child, then be sure to read Chapter 2 in its entirety. You will need to discuss a proposed parenting plan with your divorce attorney and form a strategy early in the case.

I devote **Chapter 3 — *All About Finances: Ready for Child Support or Spousal Maintenance?* —** to the economic and financial aspects of divorce. So you can begin preparing your case to the greatest extent possible before the divorce petition is even filed, I provide pre-filing instructions to better protect your rights and interests.

I first discuss child support and how to go about calculating the amount each parent is expected to contribute under the *Arizona Child Support Guidelines.*

Secondly, I discuss statutory eligibility for spousal maintenance and the key factors to consider when determining an amount to award the supported spouse. Maintenance calculations lack the predictability of mandatory guidelines, but many couples reach agreement on this issue and include terms in their separation agreement. Whatever lifestyle was enjoyed during the marriage, Chapter 3 will help you prepare your post-divorce financial picture.

I cover the disposition of property in **Chapter 4 — *Property Division: Who Gets What and Why?*** Among other things, division of marital property includes splitting 50/50 the parties' community assets, tangible and intangible. Marital property includes pensions, military retired pay, IRAs, and 401(k)s, too. I also talk about what to do if you want to remain in the family home when it is a marital asset that must be divided in the divorce.

To understand how your assets and debts will be divided in the proceedings, you need to learn how to identify *separate property* and *community property* — the two are treated very differently in Arizona law. Classifying property can be made even more challenging where *commingling* or *transmutation* occurred to change a separate asset into something community-owned.

You and your spouse will be negotiating a *separation agreement* in the divorce, which means good faith efforts to reach a property settlement are expected. Whether by agreement or judicial determination at trial, an essential component of any fair and reasonable property distribution plan is *valuation*. Chapter 4 will guide you through the valuation process of various kinds of assets, too.

My discussion in **Chapter 5 — *Privacy and Security: Why Should You Take Action?* —** continues to gain importance in pending divorce and child custody cases. New technology only amplifies the need for you to take intentional steps to preserve your privacy and protect your security at home, at work, and elsewhere.

Subjects you must learn about include, first, the risks associated with social media networking (yes, posting user content and images on websites really does involve risk). And second, the necessity of protecting personally identifiable information (PII). Learn to be vigilant in keeping your email and internet communications both private and secure.

Along with increased social media evidence in family court, learn why securing personal information during divorce proceedings is so important. You and your spouse may be living separately, but both of your online activities will still be scrutinized. Chapter 5 provides practical measures allowing you to immediately protect all your personal accounts, online credentials, logins, and passwords.

What's next? You will need to search for the right divorce lawyer to represent you, someone you can trust and connect with. In **Chapter 6 — *Choosing an Attorney: What Credentials and Experience to Look For?* —** I explain what characteristics you should seek-out in an attorney before deciding to hire. Your future and the future of your children will depend in large part on the legal counsel you choose to represent your interests and protect your rights.

Cost is always a factor to consider, of course, but there is more to divorce representation than discounted services and reduced hourly rates. If there is one instance where "penny wise and pound foolish" is a fitting maxim, this is it. What you might save at the beginning could cost you more later in much higher legal fees. There is also the real possibility of substantive losses during the divorce that are simply not recoverable.

Divorce changes everything. The process of moving on with your life after the decree is entered will have its own challenges. Thoughtful preparation will help you make that transition, too.

I wrote **Chapter 7 — *Life After Divorce: Envisioning What Your New Life Will Be Like*** — because no divorce exists in a vacuum. Life goes on, yet in a very different direction. What will that future be like? You hold the controls. If desiring equal parenting time, then will it mean giving up a full-time job with frequent out-of-state travel in order to make that possible? You may want to remain in the marital home, but can you afford the mortgage on one income? Your divorce strategy should be based upon what you really want and what is reasonably obtainable. Try to be pragmatic.

Reflecting on what day-to-day life could be like when you are single once again will help you make choices and decisions in divorce proceedings. Chapter 7 is all about setting goals, starting a new life for yourself, creating an estate plan, making your new home your child's home, and much more. Letting go is easier when you've taken enough time to think, reflect, and make a plan.

1

DIVORCE
Making the Most Difficult Decision and Carrying It Out

The first step you take in the divorce process may be the most difficult — that is, making the decision to end your marriage. You may have reached a level of frustration so intolerable that you find yourself saying with certainty and conviction, "This marriage cannot go on, I am finished with it." Perhaps you have tried — and tried again for the sake of your children — to remain with your spouse, but nothing meaningful ever seems to change for the better.

Maybe your children are grown and on their own. It's just the two of you now with nothing in common, two separate lives simply existing in the same household. Perhaps you have stayed in a loveless relationship for far too long, and now you simply want out. Or maybe you are just plain tired of it all. Tired of the arguments, the deceitfulness, the absenteeism, the behavior.

When one spouse files for divorce while the other spouse desires to remain married, the dissolution process still continues. This is not to say attempts at reconciliation are not encouraged, they most certainly are. For instance, following service of process on the respondent-party or acceptance of process, there is a mandatory 60-day cooling off period before the court can enter a final decree of dissolution.[1] So long as one spouse believes the marriage is *irretrievably broken*, though, the divorce will go forward in the family court system.

You have likely been through many struggles in your marriage. Despite whatever circumstances brought you to this point, to the brink of divorce, now is not the time for impulsiveness. Now is the time for calm, thoughtful, rational planning and clear-headedness. Control your emotions. Focus your attention on what is necessary to get through the divorce with the best possible outcome. Envision the future you want for yourself and for your children. Keep those long-term goals foremost in mind throughout the entire dissolution process. When you have clearly-defined goals, you will not miss out on opportunities to achieve them.

How Do Legal Separation and Annulment Differ from Divorce?

Instead of divorce, could legal separation or annulment be the answer? Asking about legal alternatives is a positive step, you should investigate all possibilities. Let me brief you on these proceedings, as both are referenced in later chapters. Before going further, I am not referring to religious annulment here. On the contrary, I am talking about annulment proceedings to challenge the legal validity of the marriage contract. (Communicate with your pastor, priest, or spiritual advisor regarding any religious declaration of annulment by a church tribunal.)

Decree of Legal Separation

Legal separation is available to spouses who desire to live independently of each other without dissolving the civil marriage contract — they stay married. As already mentioned, only one spouse needs seek divorce for the court to order it. Not so with legal separation.

For the family law judge to enter a *decree of legal separation*, the respondent-spouse cannot object to remaining married despite living separately and apart or the marriage being irretrievably broken.[2] In other words, spouses need to be like-minded on obtaining legal separation in lieu of divorce. Should either party object to legal separation then the court cannot proceed further on that petition. The spouses either get divorced or decide to remain married.

Beyond that, court proceedings for legal separation mirror those for divorce in all other respects, from disposition of marital property to co-parenting a minor child. Because the decree leaves the marriage contract intact, neither party is free to marry someone else. Nor will the decree of legal separation prevent either spouse from seeking a divorce in the future. Most petitions for legal separation are amended, or converted, to continue as marital dissolutions. Still, legal separation is a reasonable alternative for some couples and worthy of careful consideration.

Decree of Annulment

Do grounds for annulment exist? Annulment is based on grounds the couple's "marriage" was never valid to begin with. As a consequence of some legally recognized defect, the marriage is either void or voidable.[3] The void marriage is a nullity from the start (for example, plural marriages are void as constitutionally prohibited in Arizona).[4] Court proceedings are necessary to annul the voidable marriage (for example, married under duress and against one's will). In cases where parties have minor children, custody will be determined and child support established. Once a *decree of annulment* is entered by the court, divorce is neither necessary nor available — there is no marriage to dissolve. Given the vast majority of marriages are valid, legal annulment proceedings are rare.

The seriousness of a break-up is no lesser with legal separation or annulment than it is with divorce. Every situation and every relationship are unique.

Collaborative Law Process in Family Law

Many couples are choosing an alternative dispute resolution path, one that allows them greater control over the outcome. The process I refer to is *collaborative law*,[5] a settlement approach being utilized more and more in domestic relations cases between spouses or parents who, with their collaborative lawyers' assistance, really want to work together on reaching agreements on all the issues.

Collaborative law proceedings are intended from the outset to resolve specific matters without judicial intervention. In other words, the parties intend to collaborate — work as a team — on resolving the matter, dispute, problem, claim, or issue before them without ever going to a judge. Unlike mediation, the court cannot order parties into collaborative proceedings.

Collaborative divorce is not for everyone, but it can be a good fit for some. You and your spouse have the option of trying this approach. Importantly, *if the collaborative process is terminated for any reason, then the collaborative lawyers who represented the spouses cannot represent them in the ensuing litigation.*

Should you be interested in collaborative divorce, when searching for an attorney to represent you be sure to ask whether he or she even practices collaborative law. Some do, some do not.

How Do People Handle the Emotional Aspects of Divorce?

I know from experience that family law cases can be extremely emotional for the parties and for their children. Everyone reacts differently to the pressures of divorce, but most people will experience some feelings of frustration, anxiety, sadness, grief, mild depression, and anger. For some, the intense emotions caused by divorce are almost palpable and may even be traumatic. And for others, circumstances in the home may erode to the point of volatility which can result in acts of domestic violence.

To get the results you hope for, approach the divorce process with a balanced state of mind. To maintain that balance, take precautions to minimize the impact of any emotional reactions stemming from your divorce. If counseling will help you get through this turbulent period in your life, then find a counselor sooner rather than later.

Have You Tried Marriage Counseling as a Couple?

Someone in your circle has probably already suggested that you and your spouse attempt to reconcile differences with the help of a professional *marriage counselor*. Marriage counseling, or couples counseling, can assist spouses in exploring the possibility of reconciliation and may guide them through their current domestic impasse. Did you know that Superior Court Conciliation Services offers free marriage counseling to many Arizona couples? Either spouse may file a "Petition for Conciliation Counseling" to request this family service regardless of whether a divorce, legal separation, or annulment action is already pending with the court.

The course of action the parties choose to take after their conciliation counseling sessions are completed is, of course, entirely up to them. Spouses who reconcile will have their divorce case dismissed immediately. When conciliation counseling effectively solidified the spouses' differences, they will likely continue with divorce. Spouses who believe they have made progress toward resolving their differences could ask the court to suspend further action in the divorce while they continue counseling sessions on their own, outside the court's program.

If you and your spouse can agree to try marriage counseling, then I urge you to take the recommended sessions and give that process a fair chance. Even if the divorce continues unabated, you may come to understand each other's points of view just a little better. Ideally, this newly gained insight could help you resolve custody, property, and support issues with less conflict. You will be able to go forward with the divorce knowing you sought professional help and tried resolving this marital impasse but could not. Thinking about divorce in the abstract is one thing, engaging in court proceedings is quite another.

Are You Prepared for the Emotional Challenges of Divorce?

Divorce can be physically and emotionally draining. There will be times when it depletes your finances, seems to squander your time, wears on your emotions, and requires you pull strength from deep within to do what you must. In many ways, it is like running a marathon.

Like any athletic competition, participants should train mentally and physically because the stakes are very high (your future). When there are minor children, a parent's ability to manage the stress of divorce while maintaining good mental and emotional health could be determinative in whether that parent gets the legal decision-making authority or parenting time desired. As I said, the stakes are very high (your children's future).

Starting with where you are today and how you feel right at this moment, think about what you will do as part of your daily and weekly routine to stabilize your nerves and improve your outlook. Many individuals will meet with professionals for counseling or join discussion groups of similarly situated people. Both activities help divorcing parties learn what to expect and how best to manage what can sometimes be an emotional roller coaster ride. There is no quick fix, of course, and what works for one person will not necessarily translate to your circumstances or personality. But understanding how others reacted and responded to the situations they faced — hearing what worked or what didn't work for them — may be very useful during the more stressful times of your divorce.

Are you wondering just where you should begin? Always start with the fundamentals. ***Strive to achieve a healthier lifestyle during your divorce.*** Eating healthfully, avoiding excessive drug or alcohol consumption, exercising regularly, getting eight hours of sleep every night, finding spiritual time — all will help markedly in reducing stress to more manageable levels. Understandably, sometimes it takes more than a good diet and frequent exercise to get through the intense emotional aspects of divorce, particularly when the conflict level between spouses is high.

You are going through a turbulent period in your life, a period when your ability to make decisions is crucial to a positive outcome in your case. ***Consider meeting with a divorce counselor to help you get through this difficult time.*** By participating in divorce counseling sessions early on, especially in the high conflict divorce, a party is better able to sustain a calm and clear head when the pressure is really on. Divorce counseling prepares a spouse for the powerful emotions likely to surface as the legal process unfolds.

Divorce counselors discuss specific coping techniques. These are intended to help the party remain focused on each legal issue and a reasonable outcome, without surrendering to anger, depression or, perhaps worse, apathy. With a qualified divorce counselor, the party learns to manage feelings and sensibly address what is happening in the lawsuit which, in turn, often leads to better results, especially for the children of divorce.

When there is any risk of domestic violence, divorce counseling may be essential to avoiding a violent episode. Not all emotional problems stemming from the high conflict divorce will end in acts of domestic violence against a spouse. But all too often that is the result, causing severe physical and psychological harm to the victim. Even though children are not the actual target of spousal violence, observing or overhearing abusiveness aimed at a parent can emotionally scar a child. Those scars can last a lifetime.

Consider seeking mental health counseling or therapy when emotional matters spiral out-of-control. Your financial resources may dwindle. Your job or school performance may be disrupted. But when your mental health deteriorates under the stress of divorce, you really need to reach out to people for help. You may not even be aware of how your emotional state is influencing you, leaving you out of sync with the most important people in your life, especially your kids.

I have seen many times how intensely emotional some family law cases can become, even more so when parents are battling over child custody. *Listen* when someone who really knows you tries to tell you, "You're just not yourself these days!" Take stock of yourself and take action to improve your emotional well-being, whether that entails meeting with a close friend, church leader, family member, or mental health professional. *Reach out for the help you need!*

With your intellectual and emotional focus captivated by the divorce, you may find yourself easily distracted or mentally detached from the world around you. We've all heard horror stories about the parent who left a child in the car "just for a moment" to dash into the store, only to be distracted once inside having momentarily forgotten about the child, the car, and the blazing Arizona sun. Emotional detachment and mental distraction can lead to tragedy. Put your safety and the safety of your children first and foremost. In your everyday parenting, accept that you are under extraordinary stress from the divorce. Take extra precautions. Be mindful of where your children are and what they are doing at all times.

Ready to Begin?
Start By Assembling Your Family's Information

Once the decision to end the marriage is firmly made, start planning for the legal aspects of what necessarily follows. As preparation for any divorce, here are seven "To Do" steps to get you started on the right track:

1. Prepare your complete financial picture.

2. Set up your own bank account.

3. Take precautions to protect your privacy and security.

4. Prepare for legal decision-making and parenting time with your children.

5. Prepare an inventory of all your personal property.

6. Prepare your contact list of important people.

7. If you really want to keep the house, then don't be the one to leave.

Are you ready to start preparing for your divorce? Take a closer look at accomplishing each step in the time you have available.

Prepare Your Complete Financial Picture

You will need to provide a complete family financial picture. The more supporting documentation you can gather, the better. Were you planning to move out of the marital home? Then make copies of everything you need for your case before you leave! Once you are gone from the premises, returning to retrieve financial information often leads to complications, delays, and expenses that could have been avoided. If there is any potential for domestic violence, then *do not put yourself at risk of harm* to retrieve records. Instead, discuss the situation with your attorney who will decide how best to proceed.

You will need copies of all your financial information, preferably going back at least 12-24 months. Here is a checklist of the financial documents you should copy for your case:

Checklist

- ✓ *Pay stubs and income verifications*
- ✓ *State and federal tax returns for the prior two reporting years*
- ✓ *Vehicle certificates of title and any loans thereon*
- ✓ *Real property and any mortgages, deeds of trust, or land contracts thereon*
- ✓ *Credit card and charge card accounts*
- ✓ *Insurance policies (note beneficiary designations)*
- ✓ *Investment accounts*

- ✓ *Pension, 401(k), and retirement accounts*
- ✓ *Bank and credit union accounts*
- ✓ *Business operations records*

Think of this evidence-gathering step as taking a "snapshot" of everything financial for your records. If you are unsure whether a certain document is relevant to your case, do not hesitate to copy it anyway. Leave it to your attorney to decide how best to utilize the information, if at all. When you cannot find specific files, make sure to locate the account numbers. You can order a credit report to fill-in important account details.

You will also need to prepare a *budget* reflecting your new living situation. If you are the parent of minor children, then carefully include all anticipated child-related expenses in your budget, too.

Now, you need to protect this information. Store the copies and any related documents in a secure place that is not accessible by your spouse, such as a safe deposit box that is in your name only. If you saved copies as pdfs or other digital file formats, make sure these are stored safely on a secure computer. Keep a flash drive or disc drive back-up in your safe deposit box.

Set Up Your Own Bank Account

You are beginning a new life, one independent of your spouse. To get a financial start, you need to open a new bank account in your name only. This will be a separate financial account from that of your spouse. Under Arizona's marital property laws, you may take your half of the marital community's cash and direct deposit that amount into your new bank account.

Take Precautions to Protect Your Privacy and Security

You need to think in terms of protecting your security now, so change the passwords on all your financial accounts. Change all your existing email account passwords, as well. (Always save any emails from your spouse or from others that are relevant to your divorce.)

For privileged communications with your attorney, and there will be many, the best course of action is to open a new secure email account *in your name only*. If you suspect at any time that your spouse has somehow managed to acquire your password, then change your password immediately and notify your attorney of the potential breach of privacy.

Be very cautious and circumspect in your use of social media websites like Facebook, Instagram, LinkedIn, and Twitter before, during, and after your divorce. With online social media networking, you need to take extra precautions to protect your privacy and your reputation. Your online social media presence will be highly scrutinized during the divorce. Always be mindful that *what you post may be used against you as evidence in a family law case!* My advice? Think about logging off altogether until after the divorce is final. Even after the divorce is final, however, any online lack of decorum could easily come back to haunt you later in a child custody matter.

To protect your safety, security, and privacy, you should also change the passcode or password on your alarm systems. If you do not have an alarm system in your home and are concerned with safety (even if only because you are unaccustomed to living alone), then consider contacting a security company in your area for a professionally installed home security system.

Prepare for Legal Decision-Making and Parenting Time with Your Children

Parents who divorce are required to create an in-depth parenting plan for the care of their children. Start keeping a parenting journal to calendar and note what is happening on a daily, weekly, and monthly basis regarding each of your children.

Creating a parenting plan is a lengthy process, so begin by thinking through everyone's schedules: school, extra-curricular activities, holidays, doctor visits, your job work hours, and the other parent's job schedule. Children's and parents' schedules must be coordinated and charted-out for the entire year as part of your proposed parenting plan.

You need to make decisions about who the children will live with. Will there be joint legal decision-making?

Are you seeking sole legal decision-making? How often will the other spouse have parenting time? How will the children's expenses be paid? Decisions must also be made over the children's healthcare, education, religion, and welfare. If you will not be seeking legal decision-making authority, then focus on how you can maximize your parenting time and stay involved in your kids' daily lives.

Prepare an Inventory of All Your Personal Property

Division of property is an important phase in the divorce process. To prepare, you must take inventory of *all* your personal property. I recommend that you take photographs or video record the community property, as well as the overall condition of your marital home. To prepare an accurate inventory, it may be helpful to list the personal items in each room: kitchen, bedrooms, family room, bathrooms, laundry room, exercise room, media room, garage, and so on.

In Arizona, community property includes all assets that you and your spouse accumulated during the marriage. By contrast, separate property includes those things owned by you or your spouse before the marriage, or that either of you acquired by gift or inheritance during the marriage. As you compile your written inventory of personal property, list the item description and jot down a "C" (for community) or "S" (for separate) next to each entry for later reference.

If you plan to leave the marital home, then take those things that are irreplaceable to you, such as photographs of your children and family keepsakes. Don't leave these items in trust with your spouse, you may never get them back. Instead, make copies and take photograph of the items, then place them in your personal safe deposit box or store them appropriately at some other secure location.

Prepare Your Contact List of Important People

With your life about to undergo a major change, this is not the time to lose contact with those who are involved in your family's life. These are important people with whom you need to stay connected during and after the divorce. Prepare a complete list of telephone, address, and email information for your family's doctors, teachers, accountants, financial planners, insurance agents, counselors, professional advisors, daycare centers, employers, pastors, family members, neighbors, and so on.

If You Really Want to Keep the House, Then Don't Be the One to Leave

Whether or not to stay in the home is a very important decision requiring careful consideration, even more so when you have minor children. If you really want to remain in the marital home during and after the divorce, then do not move out.

Before you commit to staying or leaving, though, take time to reflect. What is the condition of the residence? Does it need major repair? Are you able to devote the time and money necessary to maintain the house on your own? How closely tied are you and your children to the community? Is the home in a safe neighborhood? Are the schools good? Will your children be bussed long distances to school? What employment opportunities are there for you? What about listing the property for sale? If the house is sold, are you likely to make money, lose money, or break even? Is there more desirable housing available elsewhere?

A word on domestic violence. There is one crucial exception to remaining in the home during and after the divorce. Whenever there is potential for domestic violence *put your safety and the safety of your children first and leave the marital home* for a safer environment or safe house. When you or your children are threatened with domestic violence or abuse, immediately contact your local police or county sheriff.

Getting Your Divorce Education

No matter who files the petition for dissolution of marriage, the divorce process can be a strange and challenging experience. Whether you were surprised by the divorce or saw it coming long ago, the emotional, financial, and children's issues will impact you significantly. Just about every aspect of your personal life will be discussed during the divorce. Getting a basic divorce education will make handling your own case considerably easier. Not easy, but certainly easier. Once again, we start with the fundamentals.

In the legal sense, divorce terminates the marriage contract between husband and wife, giving each the right to marry some other person after the divorce is final. Our Arizona Superior Courts have subject matter jurisdiction over all family law matters including: Annulment, legal separation, divorce, legal decision-making and parenting time, child support, property division, and spousal maintenance.[6] The family law judge in the divorce will divide and distribute the parties' marital assets and debts, approve a parenting plan, establish child support, and order spousal support when appropriate.

What Are Legal Grounds for an Arizona Divorce?

Arizona's no-fault divorce law allows the family court to legally dissolve a marriage without allegations of fault, guilt, or marital misconduct — this effectively takes the blame out of divorce. Unlike some states, there is no requirement in Arizona that spouses be separated for a specified period of time before the divorce decree can be entered. And either spouse may obtain a divorce without the other's consent.

The no fault ground for divorce is very specific — the marriage is "irretrievably broken" with no reasonable expectation of reconciliation.[7] Once the no fault ground is established, the court has authority to dissolve the civil marriage contract between the parties. However, there is another Arizona marriage that does require specific allegations and proofs before the marriage contract may be dissolved by the court — the covenant marriage.

What Is Arizona's Covenant Marriage?

Additional requirements and formalities are involved when two people enter (or exit out of) a covenant marriage. Premarital counseling, for instance, is a prerequisite.[8] The couple's marriage license reflects their covenant election. The family law judge can only dissolve a covenant marriage[9] when the party seeking divorce alleges and proves the truth of at least one of the following:

1. The other spouse committed adultery.

2. The other spouse was convicted of a felony and sentenced to imprisonment or death.

3. The other spouse abandoned the marital home for at least a year.

4. The other spouse committed domestic violence or abuse.

5. For at least two years, the spouses were separated continuously without reconciliation.

6. For at least one year after obtaining a decree of legal separation, the spouses lived separately and apart continuously without reconciliation.

7. The other spouse habitually abused drugs or alcohol.

8. Both spouses agree to dissolve their covenant marriage.

Although the Arizona covenant marriage has been a legal option for couples since 1998, most people choose a traditional marriage which allows for no-fault divorce proceedings.

Drive-By View of Arizona's Divorce Procedure

The divorce process can seem rather daunting at first, but as you read through each chapter of my Arizona Divorce Handbook it will become less and less a mystery. The first restriction you need to know about is the preliminary injunction levied on parties in divorce.

Automatic Preliminary Injunction in Divorce

One of the first restrictions imposed on spouses is the *preliminary injunction* which is automatically in place at the outset of divorce proceedings.[10] At a minimum, the preliminary injunction is a court order intended to maintain the status quo while the divorce is pending or until temporary orders addressing specific concerns can be entered and the injunction modified. Doing anything beyond what the parties need to do in the ordinary course of business — as in buying necessaries and cover-ing living expenses — can violate the injunction. As a judicial order, violating the preliminary injunction could quickly result in an action for contempt of court.

Intentionally violating the injunction could also destroy one's reputation for honesty and integrity in the eyes of the judge. I strongly recommend you do not test the court's patience on this. Either obtain the other party's written consent or seek the court's permission. You do not want to violate the injunction. Self-help is not an option. Rarely do exigent circumstances justify or excuse a party's violation.

What follows is a drive-by view of the main steps you will encounter in your Arizona divorce.

Step 1: Petition for Dissolution of Marriage

Filing this petition asks the court to dissolve the marriage and provide specified relief (outcome). This pleading is the document that initiates divorce proceedings in Superior Court. The preliminary injunction immediately applies to the petitioner upon filing.

Step 2: Summons and Response

The next step starts with formal notice to your spouse (the other party) of your intention to pursue court action to obtain a legal divorce. The other party's response acknowledges the beginning of divorce proceedings. With service of process on the other spouse, the preliminary injunction now applies to both parties.

Step 3: Motions

These are formal requests for the court to order some type of action before the trial.

Step 4: Discovery

This phase of the divorce allows each side to gather information and evidence in support of their legal arguments. The parties will exchange what is discoverable in order to fully prepare for the proceedings ahead. Tools of discovery include interrogatories,[11] depositions,[12] requests for production,[13] requests for admission,[14] and the like.

Step 5: Hearings and Temporary Orders

Typically, there are questions and situations that need to be temporarily resolved before a final agreement is reached or divorce ordered by the court. If the parties cannot agree on where their children should live during the pending divorce, for example, then they will ask the judge to hear the matter and decide for them, entering interim orders accordingly. In general, temporary orders remain in effect until a final determination is made at the end of the divorce.

Step 6: Trial

This is a critical court appearance before the judge where the case will be decided. The trial may include witnesses, friends, family members, financial experts, psychologists and mental health professionals, as well as submission of other types of evidence, such as financial records, title instruments, and photographs. Although most divorces avoid trial using alternative dispute resolution, preparing for the possibility of litigation is still necessary. When parties reach complete agreement — settling all issues in their divorce and setting forth the terms in a separation agreement — the necessity of a trial may be avoided.

Step 7: Decree of Divorce

The decree of dissolution is a judgment, a legal statement of the judge's rulings on all the issues in question during the trial. These include legal decision-making authority and parenting time, a parenting plan and child support, spousal maintenance and property division.

Step 8: Direct Appeal from Final Judgment

Each party has a right to appeal any aspect of the divorce decree that is a final judgment. In hopes of obtaining a different outcome, a direct appeal seeks review by a judicial body of higher authority, namely the Arizona Court of Appeals.

Trial litigation is expensive, but so is the appeals process. Choose your battles wisely. Certainly, some appeals are necessary and worth the time, effort, and expense. But insignificant disappointments with the divorce decree seldom justify spending large sums on lengthy appeals. Filing a frivolous appeal or using the appeal process as a delay tactic could result in dismissal and being ordered to pay the other party's legal expenses and attorney's fees. All of this adds to the cost of a now lengthy divorce — emotionally and financially.

In addition to a direct appeal, there are other appeal avenues available to the parties. Although rarely granted, a party could request discretionary review by the Arizona Supreme Court. A motion for reconsideration or clarification by the Superior Court is another possibility, among other things. The likelihood of success on appeal is a question to ask an attorney experienced in family law appeals.

Reading through the following chapters, it's only natural that you should develop questions pertinent to your family's unique circumstances. To continue your divorce education beyond the pages of this book, I encourage you to visit my law firm's website at *www.ArizonaLawGroup.com* for additional family law information.

Chapter Notes

1. ARS § 25-329. Waiting period.

2. ARS § 25-313. Decree of legal separation; findings necessary.

3. ARS § 25-101. Void and prohibited marriages.

4. Arizona Constitution, Article XX § 2.

5. Rule 67.1 Arizona Rules of Family Law Procedure (ARFLP). Uniform Collaborative Law Rules.

6. Arizona Constitution, Article VI § 14.

7. ARS § 25-316. Irretrievable breakdown; finding.

8. ARS § 25-901. Covenant marriage; declaration of intent, filing requirements.

9. ARS § 25-903. Dissolution of a covenant marriage; grounds.

10. ARS §25-315. Temporary order or preliminary injunction; effect; definition.

11. Rule 60 ARFLP. Interrogatories to Parties.

12. Rule 57 ARFLP. Depositions by Oral Examination.

13. Rule 62 ARFLP. Production of Documents and Things and Entry onto Land.

14. Rule 64 ARFLP. Requests for Admission.

2
PARENTING PLANS
Who Gets the Kids?

If you and your spouse have children, then legal decision-making and parenting time are the most important family decisions you will be making in your divorce. Take a moment now to visualize yourself raising the children after the divorce is final. What is your plan for child custody?

Have you thought about what your kids' lives will be like? What relationship do you hope to have with your children? What kind of relationship will your children have with the other parent? If your child is disabled, how will you ensure those special needs are met? In the event of remarriage, how do you believe your children should be treated by a stepparent? When your child graduates from high school, will both parents assist with the cost of vocational training or college tuition?

The answers to these and related custody questions are often passionate and emotionally charged. And that is to be expected to some degree, we are talking about your children's futures, after all. Still, try toning down the emotional dial. Being reactionary will not help you get what you really desire for custody. Proving your case will.

Staying on top of the child custody issues in your divorce will require considerable effort on your part. Start preparing immediately. You need to learn about Arizona's custody laws; what the court will require from you and the other parent; what your respective parental rights are; and what your legal options may be.

This chapter starts with a short introduction followed by a description of legal decision-making, parenting time, and parenting plans. When you finish reading the Arizona Divorce Handbook, consider obtaining our parents' companion book for greater coverage of the issues — *Arizona Child Custody Essentials, What Every Parent Needs to Know.*

Introducing Child Custody

Many parents arrive at my law office with only a vague idea of what child custody is all about. Some parents have dealt with these issues in previous family law cases, but most are in the dark over how Arizona's courts handle the legal decision-making and parenting time matters that, together, make up what we think of as child custody. Not only do people struggle with the legal terminology, they are often under the misguided impression that child custody laws are uniform from state to state. This is not so!

In some states, for example, a child may choose which parent to live with. In Arizona, the court is required to consider the child's wishes as to legal decision-making and parenting time, yet only when the child is of "suitable age and maturity."[1] This is one of many factors to be considered in determining what custody arrangement is in the child's best interests. But that child has *no right to choose* who to reside with or who shall have legal decision-making authority.

Best Interests of the Child

Your child custody proceedings must answer the question, "What is in the best interests of your child?" This is known as the best interests analysis and it involves the court's consideration of many factors. The law presumes, for one, that it is in the child's best interests to have both parents participating as equally as possible in that child's life and on all levels of parenting. The parent who has a differing opinion, for instance who seeks to limit the other parent's legal access to the child, will have the burden of proving by a preponderance of the evidence (more likely than not) why it is not in that child's best interest to have the other parent equally involved.

Be mindful not every parent will get their desired decision-making and parenting time. Nor does joint legal decision-making guarantee equal parenting time.[2] Reasons for unequal parenting might be the other parent's significant history of domestic violence or child abuse,[3] or drug addiction and alcohol abuse.[4] A parent's conviction history of drug offenses in the prior year also creates a rebuttable presumption that sole or joint custody for the offending parent is contrary to the child's best interests.

The parent who is a registered sex offender or who was convicted of murdering the child's other parent will not be granted sole or joint legal decision-making, parenting time, or even unsupervised parenting time. The exception being if the court, after considering credible evidence, makes specific findings that the parent in question poses "no significant risk to the child" and sets forth its reasons for why no risk is posed.[5] This should help illustrate the strong presumption that both parents' active involvement really is in their child's best interests.

This may surprise you, but there is no presumption in the law that the child's mother should get custody. The law is gender neutral. Instead, it is the parent serving as the child's day-to-day caregiver that carries the greater weight with the court in determining custody. Nor will the court prefer one parent's proposed parenting plan over the other's because of the child's sex or gender.

Does the child have a say in this, too? Although not a common practice in Arizona, the family law judge does have discretion to interview the child *in camera* to hear the child's position on parenting time and legal decision-making. Typically, the judge will choose to refer child interviews to conciliation services, requesting submission of a report to the court regarding the child's wishes. Judges may also consider the parents' testimony on *what they believe* their child's wishes for custody are. More commonly, though, the court will be guided by the professional opinions of mental health experts in deciding what is in the child's best interests.

What Every Parent Should Know About Legal Decision-Making

Whenever I begin discussing "who gets custody" with a parent, I start the conversation with a clear description of the two basic divisions — that is, the difference between legal decision-making and parenting time. Those two concepts are the legal components of what we think of generally as child custody. You need to learn about them.

A few words about old custody terminology and the new. Years ago under previous law, child custody was divided into visitation rights, physical custody, and legal custody. Today, visitation relates only to grandparents and certain third parties.[6] Physical and legal custody terms are no longer assigned in Arizona family law cases. Here's what you need to know about current custody law.

For one, think of *legal decision-making* as the cornerstone of a parent's legal authority. The parent with legal decision-making has authority to determine how major decisions over the child will be made.[7] These are major decisions over many important matters — the child's healthcare, education, personal care, and the faith the child is brought up in. These are all non-emergency type decisions. Nor are they the routine decisions every parent necessarily makes while the child is present there for parenting time.

Additionally, if one parent is granted *sole legal decision-making*, then only that parent has authority to determine how those major decisions will be made. Under joint legal decision-making, the most common arrangement in Arizona, both parents share equal decision-making authority over these major child-rearing matters.

Parents with joint legal decision-making have equal rights and responsibilities unless specific decision-making authority over a certain matter is assigned to just one parent. By way of example only, the parent with whom the child resides most of the time may have final say on which school the child shall attend, while both parents jointly decide all remaining concerns over religious upbringing, healthcare, and personal care.

What Does It Mean to Have Parenting Time?

When a minor child is involved in a couple's break-up, major decisions over *parenting time* must be made in the child's best interests. First, the term parenting time refers to the amount of time the child will spend with each parent (hours, days, and overnights). Recall how important it is to the child's best interests for both parents' involvement. Even when a parent is not awarded any legal decision-making authority, it is generally still in the best interests of the child to have "substantial, frequent, meaningful and continuing contact" with that parent. In other words, parenting time access to the child is still warranted. The only exception is if, after court hearing, the family law judge finds such parenting time would "endanger the child's physical, mental, moral or emotional health."[8]

When talking about who has parenting time, neither party is referred to as the custodial parent. However, the terms "primary residential parent" and "non-custodial parent" do apply to child support calculations. You'll read about that in *Chapter 3*.

Second, what parenting time encompasses is the regular parenting schedule for the child (once known as visitation), as well as holiday parenting time, summer parenting time, and any other special parenting time, including vacations and special occasions. Parents are encouraged to work together and create their own parenting schedule. In doing so, they can avoid the expense and uncertainty of contested custody litigation.

Let's dig a little deeper and delve into the essentials of legal decision-making and parenting time.

Learning to Navigate Arizona's Child Custody Framework

The place to begin studying Arizona's child custody framework is ARS § 25-403 which gives the court discretion to order sole or joint legal decision-making authority as well as specific parenting time.

Before I move on, the family law judge's authority to make decisions for parents is not without limit. The court has no power to "make the legal decisions concerning a child's life."[9] When parents with joint legal decision-making are at loggerheads over their child's medical treatment, for example, the judge can only decide which parent shall have "final say." Having final say is not the same as sole legal decision-making, however. The judge cannot decide what the final medical treatment will be but may grant one parent sole authority to decide on it.

Who Can Seek Custody?

Either parent may seek to gain legal decision-making and parenting time of the child. Once a custody action is initiated, the court begins assessing what is in the best interests of the child and may award joint legal decision-making over either parent's objections. The mother or father may request temporary custody orders to address parenting time during pendency of the action, before a trial and permanent orders are forthcoming.

When parties do not agree on a parenting arrangement and custody is contested, the court must make "specific findings on the record about all relevant factors and the reasons for which the decision is in the best interests of the child."

Look to ARS § 25-403(A)'s laundry list of statutory factors when determining what parenting arrangement is in the child's best interests. These factors are relevant to your child's physical and emotional well-being:

1. The past, present and potential future relationship between the parent and the child.

2. The interaction and interrelationship of the child with the child's parent or parents, the child's siblings and any other person who may significantly affect the child's best interest.

3. The child's adjustment to home, school and community.

4. If the child is of suitable age and maturity, the wishes of the child as to legal decision-making and parenting time.

5. The mental and physical health of all individuals involved.

6. Which parent is more likely to allow the child frequent, meaningful and continuing contact with the other parent. This paragraph does not apply if the court determines that a parent is acting in good faith to protect the child from witnessing an act of domestic violence or being a victim of domestic violence or child abuse.

7. Whether one parent intentionally misled the court to cause an unnecessary delay, to increase the cost of litigation or to persuade the court to give a legal decision-making or a parenting time preference to that parent.

8. Whether there has been domestic violence or child abuse pursuant to § 25-403.03.

9. The nature and extent of coercion or duress used by a parent in obtaining an agreement regarding legal decision-making or parenting time.

10. Whether a parent has complied with chapter 3, article 5 of this title.

11. Whether either parent was convicted of an act of false reporting of child abuse or neglect under § 13-2907.02.

Now that you have a handle on the array of custody factors the judge must apply to answer the question, "what's in the best interests of your child," you are ready to start preparing a proposing parenting plan.

What Goes into a Proposed Parenting Plan?

Given how emotionally invested parents are in their children, child custody disputes can be intense. Negotiating a reasonable parenting plan may be more difficult than with other divorce issues. This is not a competition over who wins the "grand prize." No matter how challenging this process becomes, the focus of these discussions must always be on what is best for the child.

Think of the parenting plan as a guidebook or blueprint delineating how the child will be parented after the divorce. Once completed, the parenting plan will help both adults and child adjust to life after divorce in positive ways.

The proposed plan is filed with the court and must be approved by the judge. When you begin working on your parenting plan, look to ARS § 25-403.02(C) for the following minimum requirements:

C. Parenting plans shall include at least the following:

1. A designation of the legal decision-making as joint or sole as defined in § 25-401.

2. Each parent's rights and responsibilities for the personal care of the child and for decisions in areas such as education, health care and religious training.

3. A practical schedule of parenting time for the child, including holidays and school vacations.

4. A procedure for the exchanges of the child, including location and responsibility for transportation.

5. A procedure by which proposed changes, relocation of where a child resides with either parent pursuant to § 25-408, disputes and alleged breaches may be mediated or resolved, which may include the use of conciliation services or private counseling.

6. A procedure for periodic review of the plan's terms by the parents.

7. A procedure for communicating with each other about the child, including methods and frequency.

8. A statement that each party has read, understands and will abide by the notification requirements of § 25-403.05(B) [regarding convicted or registered sex offenders or dangerous crimes against children].

Arriving at an effective parenting plan is going to require careful thought, negotiation with the other parent, and a genuine desire to set aside differences for your child's benefit and welfare. When you begin working on your parenting plan, consider downloading *Planning for Parenting Time: Arizona's Guide for Parents Living Apart* from the Arizona Supreme Court's website (www.azcourts.gov). The guide is free and includes model parenting time plans to help you schedule parenting time for a child of any age, from infant to teenager.

There are also various programs, apps, and templates available online to assist with creating parenting time schedules. Do a little surfing, see what's available and what might work for you. Of course, you could always schedule parenting time using a 12-month printed calendar, marking one parent's days in one color and the other parent's days in another color.

It's All in the Plan Details, Details, Details

All the situations that parents deal with each and every day regarding their child should be addressed in the parenting plan. Details on how the parties will share holiday and vacation time. Details on which parent will have what child-rearing responsibilities. Keep your focus on the child's best interests. When you are ready to get this project started, use the following checklist of parenting decisions to be made and included in your proposed plan:

Checklist

✓ *Will one parent have sole legal decision-making or will both parents jointly share that authority? If shared, will one parent still have final say as to any one of the four tenets of legal decision-making (religion, healthcare, personal care, education)?*

✓ *How will parenting time be shared?*

✓ *Who will be responsible for the child's medical, dental, and optical care? Which parent will provide insurance coverage for the child?*

✓ *What will be the parenting time schedule for weekdays, holidays, and vacations? (Be specific.)*

✓ *How will future problems or conflicts relating to the parenting plan be resolved? Will the cost of mediating disputes be shared equally?*

✓ *How will parents decide where their child will attend school?*

✓ *What daycare arrangements will there be?*

✓ *Who will take the child to daycare/school and who will pick-up the child?*

✓ *Where and when will parenting time exchanges take place?*

✓ *How will parents ensure the child's safety?*

✓ *What steps and precautions will parents take to prevent their conflict from harming their child?*

✓ *How will each parent maintain a nurturing environment for the child that is stable and safe?*

✓ *How will the child's basic needs (food and clothing), supervision, and emotional well-being be provided for?*

✓ *How will each parent help the child maintain a positive, healthy relationship with the other parent, with other family members, in the neighborhood and community?*

✓ *How will the child's social, academic, athletic, and other activities be supported (within the parents' financial means)?*

✓ *How will extraordinary expenses be handled?*

✓ *What will be the desired relocation notification requirements of any anticipated change to the child's residence?*

As you can see, your parenting plan is meant to cover every aspect of raising your child. There is much to think about. You may want to provide for grandparent visitation time with the kids, too. Although modifications are sometimes needed as circumstances change, a comprehensive parenting plan — with all the details and contingencies worked out in advance — diminishes the need for court intervention later with the inevitable bumps in life's road.

On whose shoulders does responsibility for the parenting plan fall? In Arizona, parents wanting joint legal decision-making are expected to cooperate in creating a parenting plan — the result is a *parenting plan agreement.* If you share legal decision-making authority with your spouse, then your plan should provide a defined, predictable parenting arrangement delineating the terms of access both of you must abide by and upon which your child depends.

Absent objection, the parenting plan will be ordered as part of the divorce decree, rendering it fully enforceable by both parents. With final custody orders in place, the parties are not reliant upon each other's goodwill to maintain and build healthy relationships with their child.

As you may have surmised already, a cooperative spirit is not always forthcoming with divorce or legal separation. Leaving the child's future hanging in the balance is not an option, though. Should any element of the parenting plan be disputed, or should parties remain intransigent, the family law judge will resolve any stubborn, outstanding issues and decide how the parties will go about parenting their child. Just knowing that the judge, an outsider, could control a family's parenting decisions should be sufficient incentive for parties to work through their differences of opinion and concentrate on the needs of their child.

Custody orders are not something judges are eager to change without a show of good cause. With limited exceptions, a legal decision-making or parenting time decree cannot be modified for a full year following its entry. Yet another reason why the parenting plan must be very thorough. Only with a motion alleging a dangerous environment for the child will the court consider modifying its child custody order sooner. Such a request must include affidavits (or sworn statements) sufficient to persuade the court that the child may be in a dangerous environment, that the child's "present environment may seriously endanger the child's physical, mental, moral or emotional health,"[10] examples of which include domestic violence, spousal abuse, and child abuse, among other things. In some instances, modified legal decision-making may be ordered when the other parent has failed to comply with the decree.

What if a parent is a service member in the U.S. Armed Forces? In that instance, the court also considers the deployed service member's military care plan in determining what is in the child's best interest. Child custody matters raised in military divorces often involve unique circumstances requiring special care, as do spousal maintenance proceedings. If you or the other spouse is a service member or in the reserves, then be sure to read our book about *Arizona Military Divorce Essentials: For Service Members, Retired Military, and Their Civilian Spouses.*

Are You Ready for Parenting Time? What To Do (and Not Do)

Parenting time is the amount of time the child spends with each parent. But there is a lot more to a parenting plan than scheduling what hour one parent picks the kids up or what day the other drops them off.

During parenting time, the party has the right to have the child physically with him or her. Parenting time gives the mother or father the right and the responsibility to make routine day-to-day childcare decisions. (Routine decisions consistent with major determinations made by the parent with sole legal decision-making, if that is the parenting plan.) In the event an emergency involving the child arises, parenting time gives the party the right and responsibility to handle that situation, too.

Be mindful, a parent who was not awarded any legal decision-making authority is still entitled to frequent, meaningful and continuing contact with his or her child and reasonable parenting time. Obstructing or interfering with the other parent's access to the child may violate the court's custody order.

To stay on the right track in the best interests of your child, be sure to apply these parenting time DO's and DON'Ts each day:

DO be prompt, yet flexible, with parenting time exchanges.

No parent should be habitually late for parenting time exchanges, but some delays are unavoidable. When you cannot pick-up or drop-off your child as scheduled, communicate that to the other parent.

DO maximize your parenting time.

When spending time with your child, make sure you

engage in meaningful activities. Be intentional with the time you spend together by planning ahead. Arrange for both structured and unstructured age-appropriate activities. If you do not obtain equal parenting time, for whatever reason, then maximizing the parenting time you do have becomes even more important.

DO make your home your child's home.

Children need a place of their own to feel secure and in control. If possible, provide the child with a separate bedroom or special personal space somewhere in your home. Perhaps a corner desk in a shared bedroom or an area in the living room just for the child's toys, books, and furniture.

DO help your child establish friends in the neighborhood.

Encourage your child's involvement in the neighborhood community and in school. Establish normal daily, weekly, and monthly routines. Children feel more in control when they know what is expected of them and what to expect from others.

DO keep a parenting journal.

Keep accurate, detailed records of your parenting time (dates, times, activities, and events). Record information about your interactions with the other parent. A parenting journal will be very useful in refreshing your memory should a custody problem or dispute arise. Many parents also keep scrapbooks, a great way to save small items of memorabilia and a sure way to revive one's memory later.

DO share information with the other parent.

Parents must share critical information, such as telephone numbers and addresses. Volunteer information regarding your child's educational, medical, religious, and extracurricular activities. Always document these events and activities in your parenting journal.

DO maintain telephone access with your child.

Maintain daily telephone communication with your child. Establish a set time to call your child and consistently call every day at that agreed upon time. If you have the child with you for parenting time, allow the child to have frequent, private, meaningful telephone conversations with the other parent.

Now look at a few DON'Ts:

DON'T be carefree about significant others.

Be circumspect and use considerable discretion when introducing any significant other to your child. Most child custody evaluators caution against introducing new parental figures into a child's life prematurely.

DON'T engage in parental alienation.

Parental alienation occurs when a parent engages in conduct that attempts to negatively influence the child toward the other parent. In child custody litigation, there is no bigger mistake than to engage in this conduct.

DON'T use your child as a messenger or case manager.

A child should never be told to deliver messages to the other parent or to spy on the other parent. Don't interrogate your child over the other parent's activities either. Don't allow the child to arrange parenting time, change parenting time, or cancel parenting time — your child is not a case manager.

DON'T confuse parenting time with child support.

Parenting time is not contingent upon the payment of child support. This may seem counterintuitive, but a parent's failure to make timely child support payments or accumulate child support arrears does not diminish his or her parenting time rights in any way. You will read more about this in *Chapter 3*'s discussion of child support.

What Happens When Custody Orders Are Violated?

Once a parenting plan is established with orders entered, what could happen if a parent deviates significantly from the parenting plan's terms? There are many ways one parent or both parents can violate legal decision-making and parenting time orders.

Maybe one parent refuses to drive the child to the other parent's home on Sunday evenings as required by the plan's exchange rules. Perhaps the party keeps the child through Thanksgiving when it is the other parent's turn under the holiday schedule. Or maybe a parent obstructs the other's frequent communication with the child by refusing to allow telephone calls as arranged.

Always bear in mind how deviating from the parenting plan is a deviation from the court's orders — a choice that could be costly. When the judge's parenting time or legal decision-making orders are violated, the court may find the violating parent in contempt, may order recovery of any missed parenting time, and may assess court costs, civil penalties, and attorney fees against the violator. Judges frequently order parties back into mediation to resolve their conflicts, too, and can assess the cost of mediation against the violating parent.

In some custody cases, parents clash continuously over seemingly every aspect of implementing their parenting plan and violations result. In other cases, there may be domestic violence, substance abuse, and other issues that interfere with co-parenting. If the court has already entered legal decision-making or parenting time orders, then there is an alternative dispute resolution (ADR) option in addition to ordering the parents back into mediation — that is, parenting coordination.

Child Custody Evaluations, Mediation, and Parenting Coordination

Given child custody is among the most contentious areas of family law, there is a distinct possibility your divorce could involve disputed legal decision-making or parenting time issues. (Even if you and your spouse seem to agree now, there is always the potential for disagreement later.) When conflict or staunch non-communication between parents becomes a barrier to cooperation when making key decisions about their child's future, it is time to bring in a dispute resolution facilitator to help break through the impasse.

In the divorce, expect input from various custody professionals whose roles are to assist parties in developing a parenting plan that is best for the child and serves each parent's independent interests. After custody orders are entered, the parties may need guidance and ADR so they can co-parent successfully under their plan. In one instance, the professional will assist after the parenting plan is ordered. Any one of the following dispute resolution facilitators, or all of them, may be engaged in your custody matter: Child custody evaluator, mediator, and parenting coordinator.

Why a Child Custody Evaluator?

In an instance wherein custody issues need greater understanding, either parent may request the court order a custody evaluation or the court may order an evaluation on its own motion when deemed to be in the child's best interests.[11] The court may refer an evaluation to conciliation services. Parents may agree to a private child custody evaluator, too. Regardless, these assessments are in-depth, typically taking 90 days or more to complete.

After thorough investigation and inquiry, the child custody evaluator provides a professional opinion and report to help parents and the court with legal decision-making and parenting time determinations. For the purpose of making recommendations in the best interests of the child, the evaluator interviews both parents, the child, and other family members, and reviews documents and records regarding the child. After assessing the data collected, the evaluator submits a detailed report to the court with recommendations.

The evaluator's function in the custody case is advisory only. He or she never makes final determinations regarding the child, that is solely the judge's role. Should a custody trial become necessary, however, be mindful that the evaluator's report will be very influential with the court.

Why a Mediator?

Mediation may be ordered in those family law cases where legal decision-making or parenting time is disputed.[12] Why? Because child custody mediation has been proven to work for a lot of people. Mediation is a confidential ADR process with a neutral facilitator, the mediator, who also reports back to the court on agreements and remaining points of contention. The direction of custody proceedings gets clarified with mediation, even if complete agreement is unobtainable, even if the process galvanizes the parties' positions on disputed issues.

Through mediation, parents attempt agreement on the disputed custody issues presented to the mediator. This could be a single issue over the holiday parenting time schedule or multiple issues with the parenting plan. Parties ordered into mediation cannot be ordered to agree, though, because mediated agreements must be consensual.

When parents join in a reasonable agreement through the mediation process, it is very possible a custody trial will be unnecessary. Any mediated agreements are put in writing and signed by both parents. Their attorneys must either sign-off on or object to the mediated agreement. Absent objection, the parents' agreement is then submitted to the judge. The judge has final authority to accept, reject, or modify the agreement. Generally, if found to be in the child's best interests and "reasonable as to support, custody and parenting time,"[13] the judge will typically sign the order.

By voluntarily mediating an agreement they can live with and that is in the best interests of the child, parties maintain control over their co-parenting arrangement. When any aspect of the parenting plan is unresolved, however, the court will determine what is in the child's best interests and dictate custody terms to the parents. To help the court make that determination, yet another professional could be involved.

Why a Parenting Coordinator?

When the level of conflict between parents is so persistent they cannot implement their court-ordered parenting plan, child-focused parenting coordination may be the best course of action. The parties must agree to this ADR process before the judge will appoint a parenting coordinator to the case.

Generally, the parenting coordinator's role as facilitator is to "protect and sustain safe, healthy, and meaningful parent-child relationships." Without advocating for either party, the parenting coordinator meets with each to discuss problems implementing the court's legal decision-making or parenting time orders. The coordinator may communicate with the child. An experienced parenting coordinator will skillfully and tactfully weave counseling, parent-education, and ADR techniques into these sessions. Unlike mediation, this process is not a confidential one.

The parenting coordinator's responsibilities are centered on helping parents comply with custody orders and on reducing conflict in the parenting plan's implementation. The coordinator reports back to the court with recommendations. (Said report may contain confidential or private information.) The court will adopt or reject the recommendations or may set the matter for hearing. Either party may object to the coordinator's recommendations, but the decision is binding unless the coordinator exceeded the scope of his or her authority.

Whether your divorce involves child custody evaluation, mediation, parenting coordination, or all three, be prepared. Read as much as you can about these proceedings, the facilitators assigned to carry them out, and their potential impact on your parenting plan. You might want to sign-up for my free *E-Custody Course* which covers these proceedings in greater detail, along other key topics.

Requirement of the Parent Information Program Class

In every Arizona divorce or custody determination involving legal decision-making, specific parenting time, or child support, both parties will complete a mandatory *parent information program class*.[14] The class is to be completed within 45 days from the date the initial petition is filed and served on the other spouse. Only the judge has discretion to extend the period of compliance. For example, when a service member's active duty requires additional time for him or her to comply with the class requirement.

Why is the information in this class so important to the family law case? Everyone in the family, adults and children alike, will benefit from the parent's participation in this class. Parties come to understand the full impact the separation, divorce, or paternity establishment case could have on the well-being of their child. More directly, the parent information program educates parents on:

- How divorce can impact adults and children in the long-term and short-term — physically, emotionally, psychologically, and financially.

- What alternatives to divorce are available.

- What marriage resources are available to help couples.

- What the legal process of divorce involves and the role of mediation.

- What resources are available to help parents after their divorce decree is entered.

Statistics bear out that parents are more capable of cooperating with each other for their child's benefit after they have taken the class. The program also minimizes return visits to the courthouse to resolve future parenting disputes. Ask the Clerk of the Superior Court where your case is filed for specific details on program providers and where and when those providers offer classes. There is a nominal fee, but some parents may obtain a fee deferral or fee waiver. After finishing the class, the parent receives a *certificate of completion.* File your certificate with the clerk as proof of participation and compliance with the law.

I covered a lot in this chapter to ensure you have a good grasp of the parental responsibilities associated with child custody. Your understanding is essential to resolving disputes, avoiding protracted ligation, and reducing the likelihood of a petition to modify legal decision-making or parenting time later.

Chapter Notes

1. ARS § 25-403(A)(4).

2. ARS § 25-403.02(E).

3. ARS § 25-403.03. Domestic violence and child abuse.

4. ARS § 25-403.04. Substance abuse.

5. ARS § 25-403.05. Sexual offenders; murders; legal decision-making and parenting time; notification of risk to child.

6. ARS § 25-409. Third party rights.

7. ARS § 25-403.

8. ARS 25-403.01(D).

9. Nicaise v. Sundaram, CV-18-0089-PR (Ariz.Sup.Ct., Jan. 17, 2019).

10. ARS § 25-411. Modification of legal decision-making or parenting time; affidavit; contents; military families.

11. Rule 68(d) ARFLP, Assessment or Evaluation.

12. Rule 68(c) ARFLP.

13. ARS § 25-317. Separation agreement; effect.

14. ARS § 25-352. Applicability of program; compliance.

3

ALL ABOUT FINANCES
Child Support and Spousal Maintenance

In this chapter, I introduce two very important financial issues in divorce — child support and spousal maintenance. In *Chapter 4*, I discuss those financial issues relating to the division and distribution of property in divorce including pensions, professional practices, real estate, and other valuable assets. For now, though, let's get started with the two basic support issues in divorce: Providing support for one or more children and for a former spouse.

What Every Parent Should Know About Child Support

In the previous chapter on child custody, I covered the core concepts relating to legal decision-making, parenting time, and parenting plans. *In every child custody case, there will be a determination of child support.*[1] Before getting into the nuts and bolts of child support, I want to dispel a common misconception regarding the connection between parenting time and child support.

Parenting Time Is Independent of Child Support

A parent's access to the child is not contingent upon the timely payment of child support. This means the recipient of child support cannot lawfully interfere with the obligor's parenting time, even when child support goes unpaid and arrearages accrue.

On its face this may seem unfair, especially to the frustrated parent who religiously follows the parenting plan while the other parent falls further and further behind on child support. But parenting plans and parenting time relate to custody, and *child custody and child support are two distinct legal matters.* Consequently, it violates the terms of the parenting plan for the parent who has the child living with him or her most of the time to refuse access and parenting time because the other parent is delinquent in the payment of child support. The solution is to pursue child support enforcement measures without obstructing the obligor's parenting time.

As I discussed previously, a court-approved parenting plan includes terms and conditions governing the parties' conduct regarding each child under the plan. If one parent violates any parenting plan terms, then the other parent (even when behind in child support payments) may *protect the child* by petitioning the court. Interfering with parenting time is harmful to a child on many levels, hindering healthy relationship-building between parent and child. In a constitutional sense, obstructing parenting time also interferes with the other parent's *fundamental right* of access to the child.[2] Attempts to enforce the other parent's child support obligation by withholding parenting time will, in all likelihood, result in a contempt action against the parent who prevented access. The bottom line? The family law judge will not condone any obstructive actions taken by a parent in retaliation for the other parent's nonpayment of child support.

One more thing. Please refrain from talking about support issues in the presence of your child. Whatever the minor's age, do not risk your child equating support dollars with individual self-worth. Children should never be made to feel their only value is in the amount collected in monthly support. Conversations involving child support are for adults only — the parties, the attorneys, and the court.

How Child Support Is Calculated in Arizona

As with all states, Arizona adopted a set of guidelines to be used when determining how much child support each parent must contribute. Support is based on specific criteria relating to the parents' income and the number of children residing in the home. *The court does not take into account either parent's living expenses when setting child support!* Only the parents' income, the parenting time each exercises, and the expenses for the child's daycare, health insurance, and special needs are considered. Unless exceptional circumstances warrant a deviation from the guidelines (for example, an autistic child's educational needs), the court generally follows the amount suggested by the guidelines.

As a parent, you need to know how support will be ordered for your child or children. Because application of the *Arizona Child Support Guidelines* is mandatory in every family law case with minor children, this is one reasonably predictable area of divorce. To get an idea of the support obligation in your case and begin budgeting, I have two free options for you. One, use the child support calculator on my law firm's website — *www.arizonalawgroup.com*. Two, use your mobile devices and download our free Arizona child support calculator app from iTunes (iPhone) or Google Play (Android).

The child support guidelines are periodically revised and work well for most families. Difficulties tend to arise when a parent is self-employed or has cash-based income. In those situations, income may fluctuate significantly from month-to-month or maybe week-to-week. Otherwise, calculating support is simply a matter of plugging in the parents' incomes, answering a few questions about the child and child-related expenses, indicating how many other children reside in the household, and arriving at an estimated monthly child support obligation for each parent.

Go ahead and run the numbers through the child support calculator to see what your figures turn out to be. Try various overnight schedules for the number of parenting time days each party enjoys. List expenses like children's health insurance premiums, daycare, and any extraordinary expenses for a particular child. Have accurate numbers before you start, not mere estimates. If you enter grossly inaccurate data, you will get incorrect and useless results. Enter realistic figures when working with any support calculator and make sure it is meant for Arizona's income shares model.

Here is a checklist of information you should have at your fingertips when working through child support calculations:

Checklist

✓ Gross income for each parent (income from any source, not just from employment or investments);

✓ Spousal maintenance or alimony each parent pays or receives;

✓ Insurance premiums for the child's medical, dental, and vision care;

✓ Court-ordered child support for children from other relationships (paid or received);

✓ Expenses for childcare and daycare;

✓ Extraordinary expenses for a child;

✓ Additional education expenses for a child;

✓ Number of children who are age 12 or older;

✓ Month and year of the youngest child's birthday;

✓ Number of parenting time days each parent has per year; and

✓ Court-ordered child support arrears paid by the non-custodial parent.

In any action involving child support, the amount calculated under the guidelines is presumed to be the amount the court shall order. However, the judge does have discretion to make exceptions when results under the guidelines would be unjust or inappropriate given the circumstances. When exception is taken, the court may deviate from the guidelines by increasing or decreasing the amount of child support.

The court's order must include the exact amount of child support and the date payments are to begin. The family law judge will make specific findings for the official record, including each parent's gross and adjusted gross income, the basic child support obligation (BCSO) and total child support obligation, the non-custodial parent's proportional share, and any attributed income in excess of the minimum wage. The parent ordered to pay support is the obligor (or payor). The parent who receives court-ordered support money is the recipient (or payee).

A word of caution. When a child under the support order emancipates, the support does not automatically reduce. To avoid an unintentional overpayment, the non-custodial parent needs to return to court and seek an order modifying child support. With more than one child under a support order, termination of support for one child could result in increased support for the remaining child with the parent's freed resources available to pay more each month for the remaining child.

What You Should Know About Child Support Guidelines

Current *Arizona Child Support Guidelines* provide necessary structure and consistency to child support orders. Looking at the guidelines may be helpful in determining each parent's child support obligation, but there is no need to memorize the guidelines. Instead, concentrate on the guideline's essential premises:

1. The guidelines apply to all children.

It makes no difference to the calculations whether the parents were married or unmarried when the child was conceived or born; or whether the child is the natural offspring of the parents or was legally adopted.

2. Paying child support is a priority financial obligation.

Financial responsibility for a child has priority over parents' other debts, which are not considered in determining either party's share of child support. (Generally, child support is not a dischargeable debt in bankruptcy either.)

3. Spousal maintenance is determined before child support obligations are established.

This is because a spousal support award is income to the recipient and must be included in that parent's gross income for child support purposes.

4. Every parent has a legal duty to support his or her natural or adopted child.

Financial support of a step-child is voluntary, however, and is not a reason to adjust the child support amount.

5. Under some circumstances, the primary residential parent may have to pay child support despite having the child most of the time.

There is no absolute rule that the parent with less parenting time must pay support to the parent with more parenting time. Although more often than not, it does work out that way.

6. Child support is calculated on a monthly income basis.

Adjustments to support are annualized to achieve a monthly figure. This allows for an equal monthly distribution of the cost item over the course of a year.

7. Basic child support is capped when the parents' combined adjusted gross income reaches $20,000 per month; and is also capped with the sixth child.

When there are more than six children, basic support is capped with the sixth child.

Parents may agree to provide additional support with monthly payments exceeding what the guidelines require. For example, they may want support payments to cover private school tuition, travel, or youth camp. To be enforceable, the agreement to provide additional support dollars must be written into their separation agreement and included in the court's child support order.

When Do Child Support Payments End?

The duration of child support is determined by the judge, who will set a termination date in the child support order. Presumptively, child support terminates when the child turns 18 years of age and is graduated from high school. Alternatively, if the child is scheduled to graduate from high school at age 19, then support terminates the month of anticipated graduation. When a minor child marries or is otherwise emancipated, the parents' obligation to pay child support also terminates.

If there is more than one child on the child support order, support orders do not automatically dissolve on the child's birthday or high school graduation day as set forth in the order. Instead, the parent must go back to court and request termination of child support for that child. To avoid over-paying, consider initiating termination proceedings a couple months in advance of the support order's end-date for that child.

Severely Disabled Adult-Children

There is one circumstance wherein the court may order a parent to continue paying support into the child's adulthood. For the court to order such support, the adult-child must have "severe mental or physical disabilities as demonstrated by the fact that the child is unable to live independently and be self-supporting." The said disability must have manifested during the child's minority.[3]

If the disabled child was already an adult when the divorce was filed or will be an adult by the time the final decree is issued, then the parent may still seek the child support order. There is no requirement that the parent obtain a custody or guardianship order before the court can order support for a disabled adult-child.[4] In these special circumstances, the court may order support paid to the adult-child directly or to the parent providing the needed care.

What About Child Support Enforcement?

In Arizona, the parent who fails to financially support his or her minor child will be penalized. If the obligor-parent falls behind on child support payments, then the appropriate course of action is to seek lawful enforcement of the order. This means filing a petition to enforce the support order with the court. For child support cases administered under Title IV-D of the Social Security Act, the Arizona Department of Economic Security's Child Support Enforcement office pursues most parents' claims for past due support, or arrearages.

Consequences of Violating Child Support Orders

Being found in violation of the court's child support order will have consequences. The court in contempt proceedings may order the violating parent jailed and fined. The judge may suspend the violator's driver's license, professional or occupational license, and recreational license or permit. To get the missing funds, the court may seize the violating parent's assets and intercept state tax refunds. A judgment for child support arrearages also accrues interest, currently 10% per year in Arizona.[5] There is no statute of limitations on arrears, so court action to collect unpaid support could come long after the child's high school graduation. Realistically, the longer a parent delays seeking enforcement of the child support order, the more difficult collection of arrears and interest will likely become.

Was non-payment deliberate? That's even worse. Any parent who "knowingly fails to furnish reasonable support" for the child may be prosecuted for a Class 6 felony under Arizona law.[6] Furthermore, federal prosecution for willful non-payment of child support is possible when the non-paying parent and the child reside in a different states.[7] Punishment under the *Child Support Recovery Act* as amended includes a fine, imprisonment, and mandatory restitution for so-called deadbeat parents.

Obviously, some parents miss payments because of circumstances beyond their control. Such is the case with involuntary unemployment or underemployment, for instance, or an injury accident that incapacitates or disables a parent. In any number of situations, the better course is to petition the court for modified child support orders. Either parent may seek a reduction to the obligor's monthly support payments with a payment plan that allows the recipient to recover arrears with interest. If the court modifies its order after hearing, then the effective date of the reduced monthly amount typically relates back to the date the petition was filed but no earlier.

You may feel strongly that your job as a parent includes ensuring that the obligor meets all child support obligations. After all, your child's welfare is jeopardized whenever support payments are insufficient, chronically late, or missing altogether. Although you should pursue court enforcement of the support order, always remem-ber *you are not the enforcer*. However, that is not to say you should simply stand by and watch arrearages increase.

Non-payment of support is a serious problem and must be dealt with. Pursue legal channels to get those child support dollars flowing again. Make detailed notes in your parenting journal of missed payments, insufficient payments, or NSF checks when payments come directly from the other parent and not through the Arizona Support Payment Clearinghouse. Then contact your attorney about initiating court action to enforce the support order against the obligor-parent.

The DES-managed support payment clearinghouse noted above can also be used for court-ordered spousal maintenance obligations, my next financial topic of discussion.

Awarding Spousal Maintenance in Divorce

In a divorce or legal separation, the court may order one spouse to provide a fixed amount of money to financially support the other spouse. Temporary orders may include spousal support while court proceedings are ongoing with the possibility of a final support award in the divorce decree. Although some states award *alimony* to a former spouse, Arizona law provides for gender-neutral *spousal maintenance*. Such support is based, at least in part, upon one spouse's economic need and the other's ability to pay. Payment of money is not the only option. In addition to a cash amount, creative solutions might include a transfer of real property to the supported spouse, for example, or investment interest, rent revenue, a mortgage on real estate, or some other lawful arrangement.

A couple caveats. First, a request for spousal maintenance is brought during divorce proceedings, either in the divorce petition, the responsive pleading, or by motion. There is no way to petition for maintenance as an independent proceeding after the divorce decree is entered. Second, looking at the sequence proceedings take in a pending divorce, spousal maintenance determinations logically follow division of property (because the spouse's share of the marital estate is a factor in how much maintenance is awarded and for how long).

Stewart Law Group

Maintenance determinations also precede child support calculations (because monthly maintenance is income to the receiving parent).

Spousal Maintenance for a Specified Purpose

In practice, spousal maintenance is typically awarded for specific purposes — namely as permanent support for the spouse, to rehabilitate the spouse, to compensate the former spouse, or to assist with the financial transition immediately following divorce. As with alimony in other jurisdictions, all functions make sense when you look more closely at the couples' married lifestyle and each spouse's role in the home.

For one, when attorneys refer to an award of *permanent spousal maintenance,* they are talking about a long-term support award. Generally, a permanent award is for an indefinite period with no termination date other than either party's death or the recipient's remarriage.[8] Indefinite maintenance reflects a more traditional purpose for alimony, one based upon the recipient's economic dependence on the other spouse's income and resources.

By way of example only, in a marriage that lasted 40 years, the spouse who did not work outside the home — who lacks the skills needed to be self-sufficient and is unlikely to retrain for new employment — may seek indefinite maintenance for life. Social Security cannot be negotiated in divorce but calculating the monthly benefit amount is useful in determining how much indefinite maintenance is needed. To ensure the money is always there, consider a term in the separation agreement requiring life insurance on the obligor for the benefit of the supported spouse.

Now take a quick look at *rehabilitative spousal maintenance*. The purpose is to lift the spouse up with financial support in order to get back into the workforce or advance in a chosen career. The supported spouse must put forth a good faith effort at accomplishing the rehab goal, whatever it is.

Rehabilitation is about employment and creating realistic opportunities for the supported spouse's economic independence after the divorce. Consider, for example, the spouse who set personal career goals aside to support the family while the other spouse attended medical school. A party may seek rehabilitative support to help cover the costs of college tuition, for instance, vocational training, occupational licensure, or to acquire or start-up a business. Generally, rehabilitative maintenance is ordered for a certain period of time, yet long enough for the supported spouse to achieve reasonably stated objectives.

A third purpose for spousal maintenance is to compensate a spouse for investing in the marriage by advancing the other spouse's career. This is referred to as *compensatory spousal maintenance*. Take another look at the previous example. Given the sacrifices made during the marriage, that spouse may seek compensation for contributions made to the other spouse's medical school training and subsequent career. Maintenance can compensate the spouse for sacrificing time, money, personal goals (like starting a family), and career options in advancing the other spouse's educational opportunities, career options, and professional earnings.

Transitional spousal maintenance, the fourth purpose, is intended to help the party make the transition to living separately and apart. Moving into a new apartment, starting a new job, buying a new car, furnishing a different home, these are very real expenses that could sink someone trying to move on with a new life after divorce. By providing a fixed amount for the short-term, transitional maintenance provides a financial cushion while the supported spouse gets settled into a new home environment and lifestyle.

Spousal maintenance is an important issue to be negotiated in every divorce. However, there are no spousal support guidelines to follow or statutory formulas to apply. And given the broad discretion family law judges have in determining the purpose, amount, and duration of spousal maintenance, these awards lack the consistency and predictability of child support orders. Without the benefit of clear-cut guidelines, spouses are often fearful about paying too much money or worried about not getting enough money to live on.

Financial uncertainties can frustrate both parties.

Still, there are certain statutory provisions the courts must follow in determining spousal maintenance. The first step in the process is establishing eligibility under the law, which is where I begin the conversation.

Who Is Eligible for Spousal Maintenance?

Arizona courts cannot consider any acts of marital misconduct when deciding whether to award spousal maintenance. And if you were wondering, who initiated the divorce has no bearing on the court's decision either. When a party requests financial support, and either may do so, records of past earnings, work history, personal income, medical disability, educational background, and standard of living in the marriage, among other things, must be provided to substantiate the need for the spousal support requested. To determine the appropriateness of a spousal maintenance award, the court conducts a straightforward two-step analysis.[9]

Step One: Establishing Eligibility for Spousal Maintenance

What's the Reason?

As a threshold question, the party seeking maintenance must first establish *eligibility* for spousal support under the statute — ARS § 25-319(A). Whether you are asking the court for a maintenance award or the other party is asking that you be ordered to pay spousal support, the first step is proving eligibility when asked questions like the following:

- Does the spouse seeking maintenance lack sufficient property, or assets, to provide for his or her own reasonable needs?

- What property, including assets and debts, will be apportioned to that spouse in the divorce?

- Is that spouse appropriately employed and self-sufficient without additional financial help?

- If employable, is that spouse capable of earning enough in the labor market to live independently?

- Does that spouse need to stay home to care for a child?

- If a stay-at-home parent because of the child's age or condition, then can that parent earn any income working from home?

- Did that spouse contribute in a significant way, financially or otherwise, to the other's education, training, career, or earning ability?

- Did the marriage last many years, perhaps a decade or longer?

- Does that spouse's age render self-sufficiency through employment impossible?

- Did that spouse sacrifice career opportunities with lasting impact on personal income in order to benefit the other spouse?

[See ARS § 25-319(A) for precise language.]

Evidence supporting any single one of the questions above could provide a valid reason for the family law judge to grant a spouse's maintenance request. Depending upon the court's findings, maintenance is typically ordered because the spouse proved a genuine economic need for financial assistance. (Marital misconduct, such as gambling or substance abuse, is never considered.)

Whatever the circumstances, satisfying the eligibility test means providing the court with a legitimate, statutory reason to order the payment of maintenance. More often than not, a spouse seeks economic support in order to live independently when unable to provide for his or her own reasonable needs. The situation gets a bit more complicated when the spouse seeking a maintenance award appears to have ample financial resources, as does the other spouse. In such a situation, negotiating this aspect of the separation agreement with their attorneys' assistance may be pivotal in obtaining an outcome both parties find acceptable.

When the spouse qualifies for some kind of maintenance award, then check-off Step One and move on to Step Two. To determine an appropriate amount and duration for maintenance, the court must continue weighing the evidence, including when necessary, testimony from a vocational evaluator or other expert witness. The judge then applies the facts to the relevant factors set forth in ARS § 25-319(B) and makes a final determination as to amount and duration.

Step Two: Computation of Spousal Maintenance

How Much for How Long?

This second step will determine the amount and duration of the award. The family court considers all factors in the divorce that are relevant to "How much and for how long?"

Even though judges have broad discretion in awarding maintenance, the 13 factors in ARS § 25-319(B) provide a statutory framework for the court's analysis. Both parties can offer evidence during the computation process which is intended to answer questions like the following:

1. **What standard of living was established during the marriage?** Was this an affluent family? Did they enjoy stylish society with high standard of living? Did the couple live modestly, getting by with limited resources?

2. **How many years did the marriage last?** Was this a marriage of short duration, lasting only a year or two? Did the marriage last for a 15 years or longer?

3. **What is the age, earning ability, job history, emotional and physical condition of the spouse seeking support?** Is the spouse a stay-at-home parent raising the couple's children? What

jobs has he or she held? How much money could the spouse reasonably expect to earn in the current job market? Is the spouse well-educated? Would training or additional schooling realistically improve employment opportunities?

4. **Will the other party be able to meet his or her own financial needs while supporting the other spouse?** How much does the supporting spouse earn? Is he or she retired or on a fixed income?

5. **How much could each spouse earn in the labor market and what financial resources are available to each of them?** Will one spouse substantially out-earn the other under most circumstances? Does one party have substantially more assets than the other, so there is a wealth imbalance between the spouses?

6. **How did the spouse seeking support contribute to the other's earning ability and career?** Did one party maintain the household and care for the children, freeing the other to concentrate on employment opportunities and career advancement?

7. **Did the spouse seeking support lose out on employment opportunities in order to benefit the other's career?** Did one spouse put his or her education or employment goals on hold so the other spouse could get ahead financially?

8. **With their divorce final, how will the parties contribute to their children's educational expenses?** Will a parent be in a position to assist with the child's educational costs only if receiving spousal maintenance?

9. **What financial resources and property will be available to the spouse seeking support, including assets and debts allocated in the divorce?** Does the spouse have sufficient property to take care of all his or her reasonable needs without financial help? What property will make up that spouse's community share of the marital estate?

10. **How much time would be needed for the spouse seeking support to train and study for appropriate employment?** Could this spouse take vocational, college, or university courses to build a career? How much would it cost to obtain the requisite education or training to become financially independent?

11. **Did the spouse hide assets, conceal property, or commit destructive or wasteful acts?** A spouse's marital misconduct cannot factor into whether a request for support is granted or denied. However, either spouse's marital waste can affect the amount of support awarded. The court may consider any excessive expenditures, abnormal spending, dissipation of assets, and concealment of community and jointly held property.

12. **How will the spouses' health care insurance costs compare after the divorce?** What will the cost of coverage be for the spouse seeking support? Will the other spouse save money by converting family health insurance to an employer's insurance plan?

13. **Did either party abuse the other spouse or the child?** Did actual damages and a judgment result from an act of domestic violence? Were there any criminal convictions for acts committed against the other spouse or child? [See ARS § 25-319(B) for precise language.]

Having weighed the evidence and considered all relevant factors, the court determines how much money one spouse will be ordered to pay the other spouse and for how long those payments will be made. While its order is in effect, the court has continuing jurisdiction over the award for purposes of interpretation, enforcement, and modification for changed circumstances that are substantial and continuing.

Regarding enforcement of spousal maintenance orders, just as with child support, be mindful that nonpayment may result in a finding of contempt and a money judgment accruing interest at 10% per year. There are defenses, but it's a *Class 1 misdemeanor* to wilfully violate the court's maintenance order. Upon conviction, a sentence of up to six months imprisonment is possible.[10]

Spousal Maintenance Calculator

As you now know, there are no official alimony guidelines applicable in Arizona divorce. But there is something else that may help get the wheels moving. The Maricopa County Superior Court developed a spousal maintenance calculator giving spouses an opportunity to determine simple alimony support obligations. However, the Appellate court ruled this calculator formula invalid for use in the courtroom, requiring instead the full judicial review of all spousal support factors under ARS § 25-319.

We at Stewart Law Group believe this maintenance calculator is still an excellent tool for trying different scenarios and can improve settlement negotiations. The calculator could help the parties prepare and educate themselves about possible spousal maintenance obligations. Our version of this calculator is on my firm's website (www.ArizonaLawGroup.com). Feel free to use it anytime, as often as you like.

3 Negotiation Tips for Spousal Maintenance Agreements

Not knowing with certainty how the court will decide the issue of spousal maintenance is often sufficient motivation for parties to negotiate an agreement with their attorneys' assistance. When agreement on spousal support is reached, their terms and conditions are included in a separation agreement which, absent objection, will be included in the divorce decree. In addition to a life insurance policy guaranteeing payment, they could agree to make the spousal maintenance award non-modifiable despite a substantial change of circumstances sometime in the future. There is a lot to think about. Here are three tips to help guide you in negotiating a reasonable spousal maintenance award in your divorce.

1. Line Up Your Experts

Look to financial professionals for *expert witness testimony* on the earning potential and future financial resources of the spouses, namely vocational and financial evaluators. Without trained experts using recognized methods of analysis, spouses are merely prognosticating. The benefits of obtaining professional evaluations far outweigh the costs for many divorcing couples, even more so with marriages of long duration. Understand that either party may hire an evaluator to counter the expert opinion of the other party's evaluator in a so-called "battle of the experts." Alternatively, the parties could mutually agree to accept the professional opinion of a specific evaluator as part of their negotiations, just as they could agree to privately mediate the maintenance issue discussed below.

Vocational Evaluation: The employability and earning potential of the party seeking spousal maintenance is often a question for expert analysis. The professional services of a vocational evaluator who is knowledgeable of the relevant labor market may be very useful in supporting either spouse's position on what a reasonable maintenance award should be. Vocational evaluators project the recipient spouse's earning ability by assessing current and future employment and career potential, and by examining personality and interests, education, skills, training, and additional factors. They testify about current employment trends and the likely impact on a spouse's future earning capacity.

Conclusions and recommendations in the vocational evaluator's report are also useful when there is a question of underemployment (whether unintentional or deliberately contrived to receive more support or pay less money). If a spouse is underemployed and could be earning more in the existing job market given his or her field, then the vocational expert's report will reflect that.

Financial Evaluation: As discussed earlier, after the judge determines a party is eligible for spousal maintenance, the analysis moves on to amount and duration of support. The party who will pay support may argue that a minimal amount is enough to provide for the supported spouse's reasonable financial needs and that the recipient has sufficient means to provide for himself or herself already. A financial evaluator can shed light on this type of situation by using established accounting methods.

When expert witness testimony is needed, Certified Public Accountants (CPAs), divorce financial analysts, and financial planners can offer projections based upon each party's resources. These experts predict the value and return on all manner of investments. They report on tax issues, viability of income property, potential asset conversion into income-generating properties, and more. Their conclusions accurately report the money needed to continue the standard of living enjoyed by the spouses during the marriage. Maintaining that standard of living may include, for instance, the replacement cost of any insurance coverage lost as a consequence of divorce.

2. Make Use of Mediation

With private mediation any issue may be presented for resolution including spousal maintenance. (I talked about the court's mediation program through conciliation services in *Chapter 2*.) The parties retain control over the outcome by resolving issues like spousal support through mediation without turning to the court for a final decision. Upon resolution of all outstanding issues, a consent decree is filed with the court.

A *consent decree* is only possible when all divorce matters are resolved through negotiation and ADR — from custody to support to property settlement. Because the parties' agreed terms are consensual and included in a written, signed separation agreement, their divorce plan is included or incorporated into the consent decree for divorce.

This may seem counterintuitive, but mediation can represent a significant cost-savings for the parties. The fewer issues in dispute, the fewer issues to be litigated by the attorneys. In my experience, disputes over spousal support can be difficult to negotiate and time-consuming to resolve. Should a settlement be reached through mediation, at least one significant issue will be removed from the trial agenda.

3. Prepare for Temporary Orders

Either party may request temporary child support or temporary spousal support orders while the family law case is pending, even before a trial date is set. *Temporary orders* govern the spouses' actions during the divorce proceedings. In addition to support, interim orders may address access to personal items, management and control of marital assets, and other aspects of the case.

The need for temporary orders comes up early in divorce proceedings, in part because of the preliminary injunction. Problems with contributions from the other party tend to surface quickly. There are household expenses, mortgage payments, insurance premiums, car loans, and credit cards bills to pay, among other things.

Consider the economically dependent spouse who, after 30 years of marriage, moves out of the marital home into an apartment. That spouse may seek temporary support to defray costs associated with the new living arrangements. On the other hand, the spouse who stays in the marital home may need support to cover regular and ordinary expenses until a final determination is made on whether to sell the house or refinance an indebtedness. The spouses could have an informal agreement. But to ensure the other party covers a share of those expenses, the court may order temporary payments. This is simply interim relief ordered for the period before the divorce decree is entered.

Motioning for temporary maintenance orders, specifically, often initiates more serious negotiations between the parties. The financial aspects of divorce become tangible. When the judge orders interim spousal support, the amount set temporarily may also influence the court's decision on a final maintenance award in the decree. (If the status quo is working, then why make a change?) If neither spouse requests interim orders, then the party from whom permanent maintenance is sought could argue that none is needed. Pointing to the absence of any request for interim support as evidence a permanent award isn't needed either.

Think carefully about requests for temporary orders, agreements for interim spousal support, and the influence such orders could have on a final maintenance order. Although temporary, some interim orders may remain in place for a long time. From a matter of weeks or months to over a year, depending upon how long the divorce proceedings take to complete.

Starting, Stopping, and Modifying Spousal Maintenance

Looking at the divorce decree, the court's spousal maintenance award will include the amount of support, how payments will be made, when payments will start and stop, any agreed conditions for earlier termination, and whether the award is non-modifiable. Unlike child support, automatic termination of maintenance by operation of law upon recipient's marriage is immediate. The instant the recipient remarries, the right to maintenance from the former spouse expires.

Depending upon the parties' agreement, conditions controlling payment, amounts, and reasons for termination of support are typically included. For example, rehabilitative maintenance may be conditional and terminate in the event the recipient drops out of college. If spouses do not expressly agree to some other termination event (such as recipient's cohabitation) or the decree is silent on the issue, then spousal maintenance ends upon the death of a party or upon the recipient's remarriage. Is remarriage on the horizon now? If you are wondering about the potential benefits and detriments of a prenup in a second marriage, then get the facts first by reading my book — *Tactical Guide to Prenuptial Agreements in Arizona.*

Unless the final decree states otherwise, spousal support orders may be modified or terminated after the divorce is final on "a showing of changed circumstances that are substantial and continuing," as with a change in health insurance availability.[11] Following negotiations or mediation, if parties state in their separation agreement that spousal support cannot be modified, then the court's final decree will reflect that restriction.

Tax Considerations with Child Support and Spousal Maintenance

You may be wondering if child support or spousal maintenance payments could raise or lower your income tax liability after the divorce.

First, child support payments have no impact on either parent's taxable income at the federal or state level. Child support is excluded from taxable income. That is to say, the payor cannot deduct from taxable income any child support paid over the course of the year. Nor are payments received during the year considered taxable income to the recipient.

A common question is whether *income tax refunds may be intercepted* to offset past due child support obligations. The answer to that possibility is "Yes!"[12]

Second, the Tax Cuts and Jobs Act (TCJA)[13] changed the tax treatment of spousal maintenance awards in divorce decrees entered after December 31, 2018. For federal income tax purposes, spousal support is neither deductible from the payor's income nor taxable to the recipient as income. Payment and receipt of maintenance is tax-neutral, just like child support.

Third, the general rule for federal tax purposes is that any transfer of property incident to divorce is a non-taxable event. (Disposition of property in divorce is addressed next in *Chapter 4.*) With few exceptions, there is no recognized taxable gain or loss associated with transferring assets in divorce from one spouse to the other as part of the property settlement.

Before settling on a legal strategy in your divorce, always seek tax advice from a tax attorney or CPA. For detailed tax information applicable to your divorce, visit IRS.gov and download *IRS Publication 504: Divorced or Separated Individuals.*

Chapter Notes

1. ARS § 25-320. Child support; factors; methods of payment; additional enforcement provisions; definitions.

2. "The liberty interest at issue in this case – the interest of parents in the care, custody, and control of their children – is perhaps the oldest of the fundamental liberty interests recognized by this Court."Troxel v. Granville, 530 US 57 (U.S. 2000).

3. ARS § 25-320(E).

4. Gersten v. Gersten, 219 P3d 309 (Ariz.App. 2009).

5. ARS § 44-1201. Rate of interest for loan or indebtedness; interest on judgment.

6. ARS § 25-511. Failure of parent to provide for child; classification.

7. Child Support Recovery Act of 1992 as amended by Deadbeat Parents Punishment Act of 1998. 18 USC § 228.

8. ARS § 25-327. Modification and termination of provisions for maintenance, support and property disposition.

9. ARS § 25-319. Maintenance; computation factors.

10. ARS § 13-707. Misdemeanors; sentencing.

11. ARS § 25-327(A).

12. IRS, Federal Office of Child Support Enforcement (OCSE), and Arizona Division of Child Support Services (DCSS) cooperate to seize taxpayer refunds in collecting past-due child support.

13. Tax Cuts and Jobs Act (TCJA), PL 115-97.

4
PROPERTY
Who Gets What and Why?

In addition to the two support issues discussed previously, there is yet another important financial matter necessary to your understanding of divorce proceedings — the division of property. There is a lot to cover!

Starting with the fundamentals of Arizona property division law, you will learn how to go about negotiating a reasonable property settlement. I explain what it means to have assets valued. About how the court actually goes about dividing your unique marital estate with the personal assets, retirement accounts, virtual assets, business interests, real estate, and everything else you and your spouse own. Every point I make in this property chapter will help you answer "Who gets what and why?" with greater confidence.

Equal Division for an Equitable Result

Knowing how marital assets and debts will be divided is an essential component of any divorce strategy. Early preparation for a fair and balanced property award is a big step in the right direction. In Arizona proceedings for dissolution of marriage, all community property must be divided between the spouses both equally (or as nearly so as possible) and equitably.

Division must be equal because each spouse already owns an undivided one-half interest in the community estate by reason of marriage.[1] Because a spouse owns 50% of the whole community by operation of law, court proceedings focus on determining where to draw the line equitably, or fairly and justly, given the nature of each asset and debt under scrutiny.

For the simplest division of an asset, imagine a straight line down the middle of a joint bank account reflecting an exact 50/50 split. With complex assets, where to draw the dividing line is seldom easy or obvious. Allocating shares in pensions or IRAs, for instance, or rental properties and income-producing investments will require investigation and analysis, as will family businesses and professional practices, deferred compensation and commissions from employment, among other things. This is so the judge has sufficient information and evidence to weigh each factor and, thereafter, establish respective spousal interests.

Dividing the entire marital estate precisely in half is not always possible. Some in-kind distributions are typical, where one spouse is awarded one item while the other spouse gets something else. Asset valuations may be unequal with in-kind allocations. Instead of splitting hairs, the judge makes an equitable division that justly and fairly allocates all items.

Arizona Property Division Rule

Under Arizona property division law, the family court "shall assign each spouse's sole and separate property to such spouse ... [and] shall also divide the community, joint tenancy and other property held in common equitably, though not necessarily in kind, without regard to marital misconduct." ARS § 25-318(A). This is the goal in your divorce, too.

Dividing and distributing the marital estate has long-range consequences for both spouses and their children. Do some soul searching. Solidify in your mind what is most important to you. Can you envision your financial future? What lifestyle do you hope to enjoy after the divorce? Life is going to be different and your final property division will have a profound impact on the extent of that change.

Dividing Your Community Property

Every state has a body of laws governing domestic relations and civil matters generally. As you may know, Arizona is one of only nine states in the nation following community property law.[2] Given the special legal status of community property, keep two overriding principles in mind when preparing for divorce proceedings — the presumption of community property and the scope of judicial discretion.

Arizona Marital Property Presumption

There is a strong legal presumption in Arizona that every asset and debt acquired during the marriage will belong to the community. By law, these marital acquisitions are owned equally by both spouses.[3]

What does this mean for your divorce? The upside is that each of you owns an undivided one-half interest in all marital assets. The downside is that each of you shares equal responsibility for all marital debts. The family court will divide your community property equally, unless some reason is shown to justify an unequal disposition. One very sound reason for unequal division is the parties' voluntary separation agreement with their negotiated property settlement terms.

Judicial Discretion in Dividing the Marital Estate

Family law judges have substantial discretion over the division and final distribution of community assets and debts in proceedings for divorce and legal separation. With that in mind, most spouses genuinely try to avoid court intervention by negotiating their own property allocation. Their goal is to reach a voluntary property settlement for inclusion in the separation agreement.

As a legal concept, judicial discretion can be difficult to wrap your head around because of its chameleon-like character. Discretion seems to change with the subject matter. By definition, though, a judge's discretion requires the fair and reasonable exercise of power in weighing facts and assessing circumstances. This should occur without intellectual resistance to good decision-making, without bias, without arbitrariness, and without unreasonable contrariness.

The alleged *abuse of discretion* in rendering a final judgment or order can form the basis for divorce appeal. The property division will be upheld on appeal unless the trial record is "devoid of competent evidence to support the [judge's] decision."[4]

The scope, or breadth, of the judge's discretion as authorized by law depends upon the issue being resolved. Discretion to deviate from the child support guidelines, for instance, differs from discretion over amount and duration of spousal maintenance. Likewise, the judge's discretionary authority over property division is not the same as with child custody.

The judge has discretion to do the following when dividing property in divorce:

- May consider all debts and obligations related to the property;

- May assign responsibility for certain community debts to one spouse or the other;

- May consider the exempt status of property under Title 33 (exemptions for homestead, personal property, and foreign judgments);

- May order an unequal division of community and joint tenancy property, but only in the event of excessive or abnormal expenditures, fraud, concealment, or destruction (also known as marital waste);[5]

- May impose a lien on separate or marital property to secure a spouse's payment of a specific obligation;

- May order one spouse's property transferred to compensate the other spouse, among other things. [See ARS § 25-318 for precise language.]

There are property concerns over which the family law judge has no discretion, however, and must strictly adhere to statutory requirements. For example, in military divorce the court is prohibited from considering any federal disability benefits awarded a veteran for service-connected disabilities.[6] One party's marital misconduct cannot weigh into the court's property division either.

Prepare for Each Step in Your Property Division

You may already have an idea of what your separate property and 50% share of the community should be, which is good. Don't get too far ahead of yourself, though. Understanding the purpose of each step in the property division process can keep settlement negotiations productive and realistic. I have broken the disposition process into four basic steps: Identification, Classification, Valuation, and Division.

I. Property Identification

The first step requires gathering relevant document-ation and information identifying assets and debts to compile a master property list. For this list to be useful, give each asset a descriptive title identifying what it is and any unique characteristics that may impact ownership interests or valuation. Spouses will share this inventory list of what they own and owe before negotiating a property settlement.

This is just the beginning!

As noted in *Chapter 1*, you will be listing everything from the marital home and bank accounts to pensions and vacation time shares. Include everything you or your spouse owns outright or has any legal or beneficial interest in. Take this step seriously, a fair and equitable property division depends upon inclusiveness. Go to my firm's website and download our free e-book, *Getting Started with 7 Must-Do Items for Divorce Planning*.

All property interests should be disclosed during the discovery phase of the divorce. This allows the court to begin its analysis and gives parties the go-ahead to start negotiating property division in earnest with their attorneys' assistance. If a prenuptial agreement was executed before the marriage or postnuptial agreement during the marriage, then the signed instrument with any asset schedules and addendums should be submitted to the court for a determination of validity and, if valid, implementation as permitted by law.

2. Classification as Community Property or Separate Property

One of the first questions a client will ask me is "What can I keep in the divorce?" In Arizona, all property owned by the parties will be categorized as either *separate property* or *community property*. Separate property belongs to only one spouse and is not subject to division in a divorce. Therefore, classifying separate assets and debts is an essential step in determining what each party has the right to keep. (Although the parties can always arrange otherwise as part of their property settlement agreement.)

Is It Community Property?

Community property is the couple's marital property and it is most definitely subject to division in divorce. Recall the general presumption that all property acquired during the marriage belongs to the community. (Although evidence to the contrary could prove a thing is separate property, always start with the marital property presumption.) Community property includes all things acquired during the marriage, regardless of whether the asset is held in one spouse's name or in both their names. Regardless of whether one spouse took out the loan or both did. Before you begin categorizing your assets and debts as "S" for separate or "C" for community, a few exceptions to the marital property presumption are worth knowing about.

Exceptions to the Marital Property Presumption

Separate property exceptions to Arizona's marital property presumption are limited to instances where the asset was either owned before the marriage took place or was acquired by gift or inheritance during the marriage. A gift made to one spouse is separate property and separate property is not divided in divorce. For example, if you were married when you inherited your parent's Prescott cabin in the pines, then the cabin is your sole and separate property. On those facts alone, your spouse has no marital interest in the cabin.

Consider a second example. Say you retitled the Prescott cabin, transferring it to yourself and your spouse as "community property with right of survivorship." In doing so, you may have gifted the property to the community. Now the Prescott cabin is a divisible marital asset in divorce.

I bring this up now because some separate property can be easily transformed into a community asset that both spouses own. This is a common occurrence and has probably happened somewhere along the way in your marriage, too. There is no reason for panic, just be sure to apprise your attorney of the details and ask for guidance.

The separate property gift exception could also lend a hand helping a party manage expenses during the divorce. Make sure your parents understand that any gift of money or property they give you before the divorce is final will remain your sole and separate property. A gift of money or property to one spouse is that spouse's separate property, divorce or no divorce. Also, anything inherited by Last Will and Testament or intestate succession during the marriage is likewise the sole and separate property of the devisee or heir and cannot be divided in divorce as part of the marital estate.

When Separate Assets Become Community Property

As you have already seen, an asset that starts out as the separate property of one spouse could lose its separate character to become the marital property of both spouses. Everything depends upon how the spouses used the separate item while married. Were both parties' earnings deposited into one spouse's separate bank account? Did both spouses pay for the new roof on separately owned residential property?

Commingling and Transmutation

When either spouse *commingles* separate property with marital property, mixing the two things together, something significant happens. The separate property could be transformed into a marital asset in a process known as *transmutation*. The transmutation of property occurs by agreement between the spouses, by gift from one spouse to the other during the marriage, or by commingling separate property with marital property to the extent the two are no longer distinguishable. (The second Prescott cabin example above is a simple example of transmutation by gift.)

Most property divisions will involve some transmuted property. Although not exclusive to them, this is likely in marriages of long duration or marriages in which many acquisitions were made. Do not be surprised if some transmuted property is part of your divorce. Evidence exchanged during discovery assists the judge and the parties in establishing precisely when and how each asset was acquired.

When and How Was the Asset Acquired?

In general, the character of an asset as either separate or community property is determined by the circumstances surrounding the asset's acquisition. That designation is not altered because of a subsequent marriage — separate property acquired while unmarried remains separate property after marriage. When community funds are used to pay down a separate mortgage or used to make improvements on separate property, then the non-owner spouse may be entitled to *reimbursement* for his or her share of community money spent on the other spouse's separate property.

What About Dividing Debts in Divorce?

Many couples are in the habit of buying at least some goods and services on credit. Some pay all their debts at the end of the month while others carry a balance and make regular installment payments. One spouse may use a Visa card and the other a MasterCard, or some other bank card arrangement, allowing each to enter into routine transactions independently. Understand that debit cards and credit transactions do not change the character of the marital funds used to pay the bills.

When contemplating divorce, one of the first things a party wants to do is disavow any responsibility for the other spouse's credit card debts. Well, as with assets, community debts (including a tax liability) are divided between the spouses in the dissolution of marriage proceeding.[7] Just as with assets, there are separate debts and community debts.

You might (or might not) be relieved to learn a debt incurred prior to your marriage remains a separate legal obligation and is not a marital obligation you share with your spouse. This is also true with debts incurred by one spouse *after the divorce action is initiated if a decree is entered*,[8] although there are exceptions. For the most part, though, any debts that arose during the marriage along with those incurred before the divorce petition was filed will be allocated to the community. Which means responsibility for paying these debts will also be divided between the spouses.

In their property settlement agreement, parties may voluntarily classify any asset or debt as one spouse's separate property or both spouses' community property. As I discuss next, these are negotiable points in every divorce and completely on the up and up.

Why Negotiate a Property Settlement?

Every Arizona divorce involves negotiation and settlement. When resolving their property issues, spouses may freely designate *any* asset or debt, and any portion thereof, as community property or separate property. Responsibilities for financial obligations are set forth in the parties' *debt distribution plan.*

The family law judge may depart from the presumed 50/50 split of community property when parties have a separation agreement providing for an unequal division of their marital estate. If their *separation agreement*[9] is partially or wholly silent on property disposition, then the judge must intervene to resolve the dispute, make the statutory analysis, and enter a distribution determination that binds the parties.

Negotiation, then, is a very important process in divorce. As are mediation and settlement conferences. Spouses need to approach these negotiations with a positive attitude about their reaching agreements and really give it their best efforts. Recall that agreed terms for parenting plans, spousal maintenance and extraordinary child support payments, along with property settlements make up the parties' written separation agreement which, absent objection, will be included in the court's decree.

Attempting to settle asset and debt allocation issues without going to trial is a laudable goal for every couple. Despite their best efforts, sometimes parties are unable to agree on a particular concern and the disputed issue is placed on the trial agenda. Litigation is a lengthy and expensive process, one that gives the judge authority to determine all outstanding issues, including how the parties' property will be distributed. For that reason alone, most parties will go back to the negotiating table to give settlement another chance.

Negotiating a property settlement is no walk in the park. Most spouses manage the process by scheduling a series of short sessions as they work through the issues needing resolution, while meeting in neutral territory. The process of listing everything, placing an agreed value on each item, planning how each asset or debt will be classified and allocated, all takes time and sustained cooperative effort. Some couples can easily conduct a sit-down at the kitchen table to work through a reasonable and equitable property division. Other parties cannot communicate with each other on any level. Whatever barriers exist, mediation is always an option to help advance the settlement process.

In my experience as an Arizona divorce attorney, the task of dividing marital property piece-by-piece becomes far more burdensome when parties rely (and pay) their lawyers to do the dividing for them. Knowing this, spouses should always attempt agreement on property division as soon as possible. Generally, the sooner an agreement is reached, even if partial, the less money both parties will spend on attorneys' fees. Attempting settlement on the future of the marital home is a good place to begin.

Who Moves Out and Who Stays?

Negotiating to get the results you want takes some strategizing. When your spouse really wants you to do something, that's when you have negotiating leverage. For example, if your spouse really wants you to stay in the marriage, then consider leaving the marital home before negotiations even begin. By doing so, your spouse may be motivated to negotiate in an effort to bring you back. Think about this for a moment. If you were to stay and try to negotiate, then you could find yourself in a weakened position. After all, your spouse wants you to stay, you did, and now your spouse has little incentive to agree to anything other than the status quo. Alternatively, if your spouse really wants you to leave, then begin negotiating immediately while you are still in the home and refuse to leave until the matter is settled. In that way, you are negotiating for what you want while holding a stronger position.

This tip comes with one important caveat. When there is a risk of domestic violence, do not take chances! Always put your safety and the safety of your children first, even if that means leaving the marital home when you really want to stay there.

3. Valuating Community Assets

Only after each item of community property has been accurately valued will the judge divide the marital estate equally. This third step — the process of valuating assets — is a very important phase of property division in divorce. To obtain accurate valuations of your property, turn to real and personal property appraisers, real estate brokers and agents, CPAs, business valuators, and forensic accountants.

Valuating Real Estate

For very accurate estimates on the market value of your real estate holdings, consider hiring a *certified general appraiser* to assess and report on residential and commercial property values. Appraiser certification is through Arizona's Real Estate Appraisal Division of the Department of Financial Institutions.

A *certified residential appraiser* can estimate the market value of the marital home and most residential rental properties, for instance. The real estate appraiser prepares a written report with valuation of the subject property. The report includes potential uses, comparable properties in the vicinity, lot size, neighborhood land use, construction methods and materials, date of build, age of improvements, and more.

You might also seek opinions on market value from a *real estate broker* or *real estate salesperson* licensed by the Arizona Department of Real Estate. These people know their turf and can offer detailed information about the market areas they serve. A knowledgeable agent can provide useful information about other properties currently listed for sale in the same area, the average listing period up to point of sale, and the average selling price.

When doing preliminary research on your own, websites such as Zillow.com, Realtor.com, Trulia.com, and others aggregate real estate information in a useful way and are searchable for free. Although they can be helpful in gaining market perspective, do not rely on these websites for comparative valuations in your divorce.

Valuating Personal Property

When you have something you believe could be rare or valuable, do not "guesstimate" value. Get it appraised. *Personal property appraisers* of antiques, fine art, guns, china, glassware, jewelry, gems, decorative arts, furniture, and collectibles are sometimes affiliated with auction houses and antique stores. Many appraisers are credentialed members of valuation organizations adhering to a code of ethics and accepted valuation methodologies. Established organizations include the Appraisers Association of America (AAA) and International Society of Appraisers (ISA), among others. Most appraisal organizations have local or regional chapters.

With appraisers, experience is essential for accurate valuation. Collections are frequently valued differently from individual pieces. Pieces by recognized artists and craftsperson's are valued differently from those of unknown artisans. If the spouses acquired many items during their marriage, then more than one appraiser may be needed for valuation purposes.

Valuating Intangible Assets

Basically, there are two categories of property. The assets I've described so far fall into the *tangible property* category of things that have physical form and can be touched. Typical examples of tangible assets are your car, household furniture, stocks and bonds in your portfolio, vacant land, kitchen appliances, farm crops, timber, and livestock.

Intangible property, the second category of assets, does not have physical form and cannot be touched. A few examples of intangible assets are:

- Copyrights, as in an author's novel, artist's painting, and photographer's image;

- Patents, as in the invention of a pharmaceutical product and computer implemented process;

- Trade secrets, as in a chef's recipe and merchant's customer list;

- Tradenames, as in a company's branded product;

- Trademarks, as in brand recognition of a company's unique logo;

- Goodwill, as in personal or business reputation for quality and service; and

- Cryptocurrency, as in Bitcoin or Blockchain.

Always make sure the appraiser's area of expertise matches the type of asset requiring valuation, whether real or personal property, tangible or intangible property. Do you or your spouse own a business or professional practice? Look to a business valuator for expert analysis.

Valuating Businesses and Professional Practices

When the community includes a small business or professional practice, valuation by a *business valuator* or *forensic accountant* is often necessary. Spouses who are doctors, accountants, lawyers, architects, engineers, or brokers providing professional services should prepare for valuation of their practices by a credentialed forensic accountant.

Expert witness testimony is intended to assist the court in making its property determination, but the expert's analysis and report is equally useful in settlement negotiations. The business owner may know every detail of running the company, but he or she is not an accountant trained in generally accepted valuation methods. This is an area best left to financial experts.

Whether the enterprise is a manufacturing company, family restaurant, or dental practice, the business valuator investigates the financial operations by interviewing key personnel and analyzing business records. After completing an investigation, the valuator prepares a summary report of the business organization with an estimated value.

Business valuation is a specialization among accountants and qualified valuation professionals, the most prestigious of whom are Certified Public Accountants (CPAs) licensed by the state. All business valuators and analysts are credentialed members of one or more recognized national and international organizations. Among key designations are Accredited in Business Valuation (ABV),[10] Certified in Financial Forensics (CFF),[11] Certified Valuation Analyst (CVA),[12] Accredited Senior Appraiser (ASA),[13] and Certified in Entity and Intangible Valuations (CEIV).[14] I know it sounds like alphabet soup, but business valuation experience with the requisite credentials will matter when the judge weighs testimony in a battle of the experts.

How property is divided in divorce will have far reaching financial consequences for both parties. Be diligent in locating and valuating all community interests. Hiring a *private investigator* may also be necessary to locate and identify community assets concealed by the other spouse in an attempt to avoid division in the divorce. All marital assets must be brought before the court for equitable distribution. Vigilance in tracking down hidden community property will be rewarded.

4. Division and Disposition of All Property

In the final step, the judge awards separate property to the party who owns it. Next is the equitable division of community property with awards that are substantially equal and fair. Although marital misconduct is never considered in property disposition, a spouse's marital waste may be considered (discussed below).

In their property settlement, the parties may agree to an *equalization payment* of cash to balance the ledger, dollar for dollar, so the outcome is substantially equal. The court also has discretion to order an equalization payment. If a party was found to have wasted marital assets, an equalization payment sufficient to recover the innocent spouse's share can make that party financially whole again. Remember the judge's broad discretion in property division? The court has discretion to distribute community assets "in kind" (the allocation of things, not cash) where appropriate and may require an equalization payment to recover marital waste in the process.

How Are Retirement Accounts Divided?

In Arizona, income and wages earned during the marriage are considered property of the community. So are the things those earnings were used to acquire, such as the family car, home furnishings, and a vacation home. The full extent of a spouse's employment income might not be so obvious, especially with salaried executives.

Deferred Compensation as Employment Income

When recruiting talent, employers may offer executives and professionals valuable *deferred compensation* benefits in addition to salaries, commissions, hourly wages, and overtime. Derived from employment, deferred compensation refers to a specific portion of the employee's earnings set aside for payment at some future date. A typical example of this is the pension plan.

Depending upon the employment contract a spouse entered into with the employer, that future date could be a year or many years away and may involve various contingencies. If earned during the marriage to be paid after the divorce, then the non-earning spouse may be entitled to a community share. Deferred compensation as a marital asset is subject to division in divorce.

A pension as deferred employment compensation does not need to be "vested" for it to be community property. When the participating spouse has a traditional defined benefit plan, an actuary is used to establish retirement age and life expectancy. By comparison, if the participating spouse has a profit-sharing plan, 401(k) plan or IRA, then the value of the plan is based upon its current balance at time of divorce.

A different question is what percentage of the retirement plan belongs to the community — 10%? 50%? 100%? Yet another inquiry is whether appreciation or increased value of a plan that accrued during the marriage is community property or separate property. Without getting too far into the weeds, I want you to get a feel for how complex the analysis can become. For valuable assets like these, the expert analysis of a forensic accountant will almost always be necessary.

In addition to pension plans, examples of deferred compensation benefits are stocks and stock-options, bonus plans, group carve-outs and split-dollar life insurance plans. Some company deferred compensation plans are "qualified" under ERISA and offered to all similarly situated employees. Other company benefits are *non-qualifying deferred compensation plans (NQDCs)* offered to select executives and independent contractors. The IRS puts NQDCs into four categories: Salary reduction arrangements, bonus deferral plans, top-hat plans (or supplemental executive retirement plans), and excess benefit plans.

Whatever the source of earnings, whether the deferred compensation plan is qualified or non-qualified, in discerning if earnings are separate assets or the community's, start by asking "When were the earnings made?" Generally, wages are separate property if earned before marriage *and* after initiation of divorce proceedings. Those wages earned during the marriage are presumed to belong to the community.

Dividing Retirement Plans

For some couples, the retirement fund will be their most valuable community asset. If both spouses have separate retirement accounts, then both accounts will be divided. (The parties may agree to keep their respective retirement accounts intact as a settlement term in their separation agreement.) As with any other acquisition, the retirement account that was completely funded or earned prior to the marriage is the separate property of the participant spouse and not divisible in divorce unless the parties agree otherwise.

When valuating and dividing pensions and retirement accounts, be mindful that these benefits are often a blend of separate and community interests. This occurs when employment began before the marriage and continued into the marriage. One method of calculating the community share is to take the number of months the participant-spouse was married while under the pension plan, and divide that figure by the total months of participation in that plan. The resulting percentage is used to calculate the community portion of the plan, which is then divided equally between the spouses.

Qualified Domestic Relations Orders

The pension plan administrator cannot divide any pension without a *Qualified Domestic Relations Order (QDRO)*. I strongly encourage you to have the QDRO prepared early so you can submit it along with the proposed divorce decree for the judge's signature. The QDRO may be included in the property settlement, incorporated into the court's decree, or issued as a separate order.

The divorce decree establishes the parties' interests in their respective pensions. The QDRO — the court's order to the pension plan administrator — is necessary for the plan administrator to legally perform that division. With the exception of the non-qualified plan (for example, an annuity does not require a QDRO), the QDRO is filed with the pension plan administrator who implements distribution to both parties when it is time to begin releasing pension funds.

The court's Qualified Domestic Relations Order accomplishes two objectives. First, the QDRO assures the required payment is made to the "alternate payee" precisely as the court ordered. This prevents the plan participant from disposing of that share in violation of the divorce decree. Second, the QDRO ensures each party receiving a portion of the pension is responsible for a corresponding share of the tax liability.

The QDRO must be done right. I recommend you hire an experienced QDRO attorney, a legal specialist in the field. The QDRO is a very specific, often complex court-order splitting the retirement account as part of the asset division in divorce.

What Happens When a Spouse Hides Assets?

Although it is unwise and can seriously undermine a party's case when discovered, sometimes a divorcing spouse will attempt to hide assets from division. *When one party deliberately hides assets, direct action must be taken to bring those assets before the court for division.* All too frequently, a party will try to conceal property before the petition for dissolution is filed, a deceitful act in anticipation of divorce. The more time a spouse has before the divorce petition is filed, the more likely concealment of assets will occur. Be on the lookout for possible concealment in your divorce. And if you are thinking about hiding assets, well, think again.

Finding Decoys?

Were hidden assets found too easily? They could be a mere decoy for the greater treasure buried more carefully. Many divorce attorneys have observed a party (sometimes their own client) using a decoy to divert attention from the more valuable concealed asset. Say, for example, the decoy is a Phoenix bank account opened by one spouse and funded with marital assets, yet not a lot of money when compared to the couple's resources. The account is easily discovered by the other party who, having found the hidden treasure, stops looking for additional clues. Meanwhile, the well-hidden asset is a large offshore bank account held under a different name. If the other spouse stops looking for clues, then it is unlikely the concealed offshore account will be located and brought before the court for division as required by law.

Clues to Finding Hidden Assets

As part of the financial disclosures required in every divorce, both parties must complete discovery and list all of their assets and debts. If there is any suspicion a spouse may be hiding assets, then the sleuthing must begin. What follows are four tips on where and how to search for clues to hidden assets in financial records.

Search for Clues in Tax Returns

Let the sleuthing begin by closely examining income tax returns for the last five years. Study the interest income schedules in each tax return. Look for any discrepancies when comparing the itemized accounts listed on the tax return with the accounts listed by the spouse in the financial disclosure. Do they match up?

Compare real estate taxes and mortgage interest in the tax returns with the real estate details provided by the spouse. Are they the same?

Determine whether there was any overpayment of taxes which must be refunded to the taxpayer, possibly after the divorce is finalized. Will there be a tax refund?

Search for Clues in Bank and Investment Accounts

Obtain copies of all bank, credit card, and investment account statements going back five years. Examine each statement carefully and look for any large transfers or withdrawals. A pattern of regular transfers of small amounts may also indicate concealment. Do not ignore those small transactions simply because they are recurring. Dig a little deeper. How much and how often were funds transferred? Where and for what purpose was the money spent?

A spouse may try to hide cash and, on some occasions, may use the pretense of a debt when none really exists. For instance, a party may transfer money to a friend or family member for the purpose of collecting it later, after the divorce. Was a payment made to a close friend or family member on a so-called debt?

Look for any custodial account statements in the name of your child or stepchild. A custodial account could be used as a mere repository for a party to make deposits, with the ultimate plan being to recover that money after the divorce. Is there a custodial account that you were previously unaware of?

Pay very close attention to ATM withdrawals. Do the withdrawals reflect normal spending patterns? What was the money used for?

When reviewing credit card statements, closely examine the list to spot payments for motel accommodations and travel expenses. Are there charges for housing expenses outside the marital home, such as rental payments? Is there any charge that was extraordinary or unusual?

Search for Clues in Paychecks

Request payment records from the party's employer and carefully examine paychecks for any deferred bonuses, options, or wages. What if some wages are deferred until after the divorce, but those wages were actually earned during the marriage? Any such delays in paying what is owed could be evidence of collusion between the employer and the employee-spouse. A payment deferred until after the divorce would appear to be that party's separate property, unless it is traced back to the community as earned during the marriage. Is the employer holding back any of the spouse's earnings or bonuses for post-divorce payment? Is a promotion or a pay raise being stalled until after the divorce?

When a spouse is paid in cash, or partly in cash, tracking earnings may be much more difficult. Look for changes in the pattern of earnings established during the marriage. Is the party working the same number of hours, but with a significant reduction in stated earnings?

When a spouse has cash income, one way to establish whether there are hidden assets is to have a *lifestyle audit* performed by an accountant. The lifestyle audit involves comparing a party's stated income to the amount of money he or she actually spends. If the spouse's expenditures are unreasonably high given the amount of stated earnings, then the imbalance may be evidence of concealed assets. Are the spouse's spending habits excessive when compared to stated earnings?

Search for Clues in Business Records

Owning a business could make it easier for a divorcing spouse to hide assets. In some instances, hiring a business evaluator or forensic accountant may be necessary to thoroughly investigate the business records for possible concealment practices.

Wages may have been paid to family members or friends for work they did not actually perform, intending to return the money to the concealing spouse after the divorce is over. Were wages paid to family members or friends for work they did not do?

Investments can be written off as business expenses, too, and many such expenditures could be inflated to reduce income. Is the business being restrained to look less profitable? Was business equipment purchased for much more than market value? Are business expenses excessive when compared to the actual cost of operation?

Divorce for most couples is challenging enough without one party's attempts to hide assets from the other. When concealment of assets is suspected, gather and photocopy all financial records before the petition is filed. If you haven't yet separated, then consider safe-keeping those records in a secure location outside the home for retrieval at a later date.

How Does Marital Waste Affect Property Division?

My final property division topic has to do with marital waste. Before I begin, understand that these claims are often difficult to prove and are not frequently involved in the majority of divorces. That being said, marital waste is the wrongful dissipation of community property by a spouse. Should a spouse be found to have committed marital waste at any time, including pendency of the divorce, the family law judge will order reimbursement to the innocent party. However the community resources were wrongly depleted, destroyed, lost, or dissipated, marital waste by one spouse is unfair to the other and wasted funds may be recovered for an equitable distribution of the marital estate.

A party is free to dispose of his or her separate property in any legal manner, whether prudent or imprudent. But when assets are held by the community, one party cannot tap into and deplete the marital asset pool without consequences.

Wasteful depletion of marital property can involve all kinds of activities including:

- Gifts made and money spent to support an extramarital affair;

- Frivolous, unjustified, or fraudulent spending;

- Excessive withdrawals from financial and investment accounts with no accounting;

- Money spent to support excessive drug or alcohol consumption or addiction;

- Gambling losses;

- Illegal activities like narcotic use;

- Excessive gifting to the spouse's children from a previous marriage or to other family members;

- Legal fees and property loss to forfeiture caused by the spouse's criminal activities; and

- Unreasonable loss to business interests.

When property is allocated during the divorce, the court may look into excessive, abnormal expenditures and examine any destruction and concealment of marital assets. Any indication there was a fraudulent transfer or fraudulent disposition of community property will be scrutinized, too.

The burden is on the injured spouse to present sufficient evidence to support a court finding of marital waste. Once evidence is presented, the other spouse has the burden of proving there was no waste by proving either the asset was used to benefit the community or there was no excessive or extraordinary spending.

Once a spouse's waste of marital assets is proven to the court, the amount wasted is deducted from the responsible party's 50% share of the community property. If marital assets are insufficient to compensate the injured spouse for the loss, then the court may issue a money judgment against the responsible party for the balance still owing. That judgment follows the obligor beyond the divorce. In such a situation, the injured spouse becomes a judgment creditor and can continue collecting on the debt according to law, including garnishment, until the debt owed is wholly satisfied.

Chapter Notes

1. ARS § 25-211. Property acquired during marriage as community property; exceptions; effect of service of a petition.

2. The eight other community property states are California, Idaho, Louisiana, Nevada, New Mexico, Texas, Washington, and Wisconsin.

3. ARS § 25-211.

4. Platt v. Platt, 17 Ariz. App. 458 (1972).

5. Toth v. Toth, 190 Ariz. 218, 946 P2d 900 (1997).

6. ARS § 25-318.01. Military retirement benefits; disability related waiver.

7. ARS § 25-318. Disposition of property; retroactivity; notice to creditors; assignment of debts; contempt of court.

8. ARS § 25-211. Property acquired during marriage as community property; exceptions; effect of service of a petition.

9. ARS § 25-317. Separation agreements.

10. American Institute of CPAs (AICPA).

11. AICPA.

12. Nat'l Association of Certified Valuators and Analysts (NACVA).

13. American Society of Appraisers (ASA).

14. ASA.

5

PRIVACY AND SECURITY
Why Should You Take Action?

In the first chapter of this divorce handbook, I mentioned how important it is for you to take precautionary measures to protect your privacy and security before, during, and after the divorce. (You may want to revisit *Chapter 1* now.) This chapter takes the discussion about privacy and security to the next level.

Learn what a party should and should not do, especially when the case involves legal decision-making and parenting time matters. There are some very real risks and repercussions associated with social media and social networking. I discuss certain legal restraints on what a spouse can lawfully do when seeking information from the other party, including criminal spying, stalking, or harassing the other spouse. Lastly, I provide some guidance on obtaining restraining orders should domestic violence factor into the divorce.

What Is the Role of Social Media in Divorce?

Not too long ago, collecting damaging evidence against a spouse required the services of a private investigator (PI). The "Private Eye" would follow the targeted spouse around for days, perhaps weeks. Staking out places where the spouse was likely to show-up. Interviewing locals and potential witnesses who might have useful information. Snapping photographs and collecting evidence of bad behavior or wrongdoing.

Hiring a licensed PI to collect evidence is still useful in certain circumstances, but investigations are time-consuming and costly. For parties lacking the means to pay a private sleuth's hourly rate and daily expenses, the cost is out-of-reach. Collecting social media evidence, however, is an inexpensive and often richly rewarding alternative to hiring a PI.

Today, much of the work is done voluntarily by the very spouse being investigated! Admission after admission is posted to social media websites every minute of every hour of every day. Despite growing public awareness, people are seldom discrete when posting the details of their daily lives online. If a party's lawyer wants to know where the other spouse has been spending weekends, for example, then Googling a few possibilities, looking up a LinkedIn profile, making a Facebook inquiry, watching the other party's live-streamed YouTube video, one bit of evidence leading to another and *Voila!* Before you know it, the lawyer's short computer session has yielded recent results that may be useful in court as evidence.

Posting pictures and personal information about yourself on a public forum like Facebook is an open invitation for opposing counsel to collect evidence against you. Not only will the evidence be useful in the initial divorce, it is useful in any family law case involving child custody.

Using social media to network and stay connected with family, friends, and associates can be great so long as the user is cognizant of the risks associated with social networking on the internet. This should be the mantra for every party to a divorce:

Anything you post can be used against you in family court!

The party who uses social media websites must understand that content posted online may be introduced as evidence (it must be relevant to the case, of course). At a minimum, a spouse in the midst of divorce should be very cautious about every message being shared when using social media to communicate and network. Wild Las Vegas weekends, for example, do not play well in child custody proceedings.

Posting online is publishing information. Once published, the information can be gathered lawfully and used against the party in court. This means new and old posts can, and do, influence matters of legal decision-making, parenting time, child support, spousal maintenance, and division of marital assets and debts in divorce. In Arizona and elsewhere, photographs and messages posted on social networking sites are considered to be strong evidence in court. Even a spontaneous post, intended only to be humorous and entertaining, could undermine a party's case with very unpleasant consequences.

Social Media Is Bigger Than Facebook

With social media networking so commonplace, it is getting easier for divorce attorneys to collect damaging evidence against an opposing party. For evidentiary purposes, social media includes cell phone use, emails, online photographs, uploaded videos, text messages, posts, comments, blogs, microblogs, tweets, and the like. Opposing parties and their attorneys routinely look to Facebook, LinkedIn, Twitter, YouTube, Instagram, Tumblr, blogs, and other social media forums to gather evidence for use in court.

Posting anything online can affect one's reputation

in the community and, once published, it may never go away. One spouse could gather evidence from social media to demonstrate that the other party is an "excessive spender," the "irresponsible parent," or the one who is "drug or alcohol dependent." That only touches on what may be gleaned from a few well-chosen pictures.

Social media evidence might be a photograph of an intoxicated parent (establishing a lack of child supervision in a custody dispute). There may be images of luxury items like tropical vacations and expensive cars (establishing undeclared income or hidden assets when determining spousal maintenance or child support). There may be evidence that a party is LinkedIn at work (establishing earning capacity). There could be evidence of the spouse sunbathing poolside at Palm Springs during a supposed job interview (establishing failure to seek employment). All can be very damaging to a party's case.

Evidence gathered through social media may be used to refute testimony, too. When a party posts a message that contradicts a statement he or she made previously in the divorce, then the other spouse will exploit that post as evidence establishing a lack of credibility and propensity for untruthfulness.

In addition to maintaining a low online profile during legal proceedings, here are some useful tips on managing social media to protect your privacy and reputation:

- Consider logging off entirely until the divorce is final or the family law case is resolved.

- Do not post photographs or boast about big-ticket purchases and vacations.

- Think before you post. Consider the legal ramifications of publishing anything personal and exercise discretion on all social media sites.

- Exercise restraint in posting any photographs of yourself.

- When you want custody and will claim to be the more responsible parent, make sure your page reflects that.

- Do not discuss, comment, or tweet about the divorce, the judge, the other party, or the attorneys.

- When you must post a message, carefully choose your words, say what is necessary and avoid expletives.

- Do not post anything that your child should not see.

- Do not disparage the other parent or write anything that would alienate him or her from your child.

- Enable privacy settings and set them high. Even when you have blocked your spouse, a well-meaning friend may forward your post. It could eventually end up with opposing counsel.

- Search for information on social networking websites about yourself to heighten awareness of online vulnerabilities that need to be shared with your divorce attorney.

Always be mindful that something posted online is published and may be impossible to retract. All it takes is for someone to post something about you — a co-worker, neighbor, family member, or best friend. Followers and people you have "friended" can share your post and information with others. To undermine your position in the divorce, all opposing counsel needs is a compromising statement or photograph that establishes where you were, who you were with, or what you were doing.

Gathering Social Media Evidence Against the Other Party

Anything you post can be used against you in family court, but the reciprocal is also true. Evidence gathered by you may be used in court against your spouse. When you know the other party uses social media to network, inform your attorney. If you observe potentially useful online information about your spouse, then relay those findings, too. Your lawyer's use of that online evidence could have a significant impact on the divorce.

Negative social media evidence can substantially weaken a spouse's position during divorce negotiations, as when the evidence is used to disparage character or prove the party lied. Even when doing so is clearly to their disadvantage, many people will settle rather than have the information presented as evidence at trial. Why? When a spouse makes a statement in the divorce and the other party presents social media evidence exposing the statement as a lie, the spouse not only loses credibility with the judge (and child custody evaluator), but the exposure can result in personal and professional embarrassment and humiliation.

The information gathered about a party must be obtained lawfully to be admitted into evidence. When a spouse has reason to believe that relevant evidence requires collection of information under subpoena, online activities beyond social networking can be gathered from the company providing the online service. This is possible with interactive gaming and online entertainment providers, too.

Bottom line. Always be discrete in your online conduct and communications to avoid being negatively characterized in court. Better yet, stay offline until the divorce is final.

Can Internet Activities Be Harmful?

Every party to a divorce should guard against internet activities that could violate Arizona law and become dangerous. I refer to cyber-spying, cyber-stalking and cyber-harassment. "Cyber" meaning the use of computers to spy, stalk, or harass another person.

Someone spies to obtain information secretively, without permission from the person who holds that information. Spying is espionage, or clandestine surveillance. When computers or electronic devices are used to secretly obtain intelligence, the act is *cyber-spying*. No matter how naïve the party, no matter how innocent the motive, attempting to acquire evidence by spying or cyber-spying on the other spouse is a very bad idea.

In Arizona, a person may commit a Class 5 felony by intentionally intercepting another's communication, even when one of the parties to the telephone conversation or email communication happens to be the other spouse.[1] When one spouse eavesdrops on the other party by intercepting a wire or electronic communication without consent, the unauthorized listening is spying. As tempting as it may be to acquire information for the divorce by eavesdropping on the other party's private emails or phone calls, intercepting another person's private conversations without permission is a crime.

A party may successfully persuade someone else to do the intercepting for him or her, but that does not give the party a defense to the crime. In fact, it is a felony to trick, or connive, a communication service provider into disclosing the content of someone else's electronic communication. The party's mere possession of a device that could be used to intercept an electronic or oral communication, with the intent to use it, can be a criminal act.

In your divorce, do not spy on the opposing party's computer or emails. Doing so may seriously hurt your case. If you suspect your spouse has access to your computer passwords, social media accounts, or email accounts, then immediately change those passwords, open a new secure email account that no one else can access, and tell your attorney what happened.

Another criminal act is *cyber-stalking* which is using the internet or some electronic means to stalk a person. *Cyber-harassment* involves using email, instant messaging, blogs, and so on, to torment and harass someone. These are serious criminal activities. The torment can be both annoying and alarming to victims who are harassed. In Arizona, cyber-stalking directed at a specific individual is a form of intentional criminal harassment and a Class 1 misdemeanor.[2] Such harassment can involve any of the following intentional acts committed by one spouse against the other:

- Anonymously or otherwise contacting, communicating, or causing a communication with the other spouse by verbal, electronic, mechanical, telegraphic, telephonic, or written means in a manner that harasses.

- Continuing to follow the other spouse in or about a public place for no legitimate purpose after being asked to desist.

- Repeatedly committing an act or acts that harass the other spouse.

- Surveils (or causes another person to surveil) the other spouse for no legitimate purpose.

- On more than one occasion, making a false report to a law enforcement, credit agency, or social service agency.

- Interfering with the delivery of any public or regulated utility to the other spouse.
  [See ARS § 13-2921(A) for precise language.]

Orders of protection and other restraining orders are often sought in domestic violence cases in Arizona and elsewhere. The victim may also seek a restraining order from the court to stop the other spouse's stalking and harassment. If the judge's order of protection or injunction against harassment is violated, then the defendant-spouse may be charged with a Class 6 felony for aggravated harassment. Repeated harassment may be more severely punished as a Class 5 felony.[3]

When Domestic Violence Is Part of Divorce

If the opposing party is violent with you or your children, or threatens violence, then a restraining order is necessary to keep him or her away. Animals may also be protected under this judicial order. A court's order of protection prevents the defendant-spouse from contacting the protected spouse and any other protected person at home or at work. Typically, the order of protection is granted *ex parte*.

This type of restraining order is available when there is an act of domestic violence or threat of domestic violence against a family member, and "family" is broadly interpreted. For an order of protection, a familial or intimate relationship is necessary between the victim and the defendant. That family relationship includes a spouse, former spouse, blood relative, someone who lives with or lived with the person, the father or mother of the unborn child, and someone in a current or past romantic relationship with the person.

If at any time you or your child is a victim of domestic violence, then immediately file a petition with the court for an order of protection against the abusive spouse. When a domestic violence crime has occurred, supporting evidence, dates, and testimony about the violent event is necessary for the court to issue the order.

In making a decision, the judge may ask the petitioner:

1. Whether the defendant should be ordered to stay away from the petitioner's workplace.

2. Whether the defendant should be prohibited from possessing a firearm.

3. Whether the defendant should be barred from the petitioner's home.

4. Whether there are others who should also be included in the protective order as "protected parties."

The filing spouse must swear that the information provided in the petition is true and then signs its. After the judge signs the order, the defendant must be properly served with both the petition and the order. Law enforcement will serve the defendant for free (same as with an injunction against harassment). For a fee, a private process server will carry out service. The protective order is effective for one year beginning when the defendant is served.

The protected spouse, as well as any other protected person, should keep the order on his or her person at all times. If the defendant who has not yet been served shows up where the protected person is, then the police should be called and presented with a copy of the restraining order when they arrive. The officer will then serve the order on the defendant. If the defendant violates the order of protection after having been served, then he or she has committed a crime and will be arrested. Even with an order of protection in effect, the protected spouse should take every safety precaution possible and prudent under the circumstances.

An order of protection requires the defendant stay away and remain out of contact with the protected person. Although the order is valid for a year, it can be modified or quashed (dismissed) by the court. Be mindful, the defendant can be arrested for violating the protective order even when it was the protected person who initiated the contact. The court may also order that the defendant not possess, receive, or purchase firearms or ammunition, and can order the surrender of firearms to law enforcement upon service of the protective order.

What should you do? Keep a diary, journal, or log of events with dates and descriptions of any incidents relevant to your case involving potential or actual violence, threats of violence, stalking, and harassment. In detail, describe specific examples of your spouse's poor judgment, alcohol or drug abuse, violent behavior, or threats of violence. Take notes about conversations you have with your spouse over issues in the divorce. Also save copies of all emails or written exchanges with your spouse. But remember...

Never take chances with your safety or your child's safety.

If you are in danger, DIAL 911.

Chapter Notes

1. ARS § 13-3005: Interception of wire, electronic and oral communications; installation of pen register or trap and trace device; classification; exceptions.

2. ARS § 13-2921. Harassment; classification; definition.

3. ARS § 13-2921.01. Aggravated harassment; classification; definition.

6

CHOOSING AN ATTORNEY
What Should You Look For?

In Arizona, you are not required to hire an attorney to represent you in the divorce. So the first question you should ask yourself is whether you will hire an attorney or not. Understand that as soon as the petition for dissolution of marriage and responsive pleading are filed with the Clerk of the Superior Court, the spouses become "parties" to a legal action in which their respective interests are often in opposition.

Many couples may think they are better off saving money by simply sharing legal fees and hiring one attorney to represent the them both. I offer a few words of caution against attempting to share one divorce attorney between the two of you. Not only would this violate the professional ethical standards required of the attorney who is only permitted to work with one party in a divorce, it would jeopardize one and possibly both spouse's legal rights and interests. There is a direct conflict of interest in such dual representation.

In some instances, one spouse may hire an attorney while the other spouse represents himself or herself *in propria persona*, or *pro se*. That does not present an ethical issue for the divorce attorney because the legal representation is limited to one spouse. However, the attorney will be advocating on behalf of his or her client only and not the pro se party. In many instances, and depending upon the complexity of the circumstances, it may be best to hire a divorce attorney to take control and drive the case to conclusion.

If you are unsure whether to hire any attorney at all, then take a moment to investigate what is involved in the do-it-yourself divorce. You may find that this is something you could accomplish on your own if the requisite divorce resources were made available to you. Many people prefer to do the legal work themselves for a variety of reasons, but it is no panacea and does not work for everyone. When done correctly, the self-service divorce often represents a significant savings on attorneys' fees. If the pro se party is not fully prepared for every legal proceeding, then the do-it-yourself divorce can cause substantial legal problems (which may or may not be correctable) and cost even more later in attorneys' fees over damage control.

8 Questions to Ask the Divorce Attorney

Once the decision to hire a divorce attorney is made, the next serious task is selecting the right person to represent you. Choosing your attorney may be one of the most important decisions you will ever make. Without question, you want the most favorable results possible for yourself and for your children. Of course you need to know how much you will be charged, but you should not base your hiring decision on legal fees alone.

The more selective you are in choosing a divorce attorney, the more confidence you will have in the representation and in the legal proceedings. The last thing you need at this time is increased anxiety stemming from a lack of confidence in your attorney and concern over the legal merits of your case!

Most importantly, you want to hire an experienced attorney. One who is capable of guiding you through the entire divorce process efficiently and expertly. Before making that hiring decision, get candid answers to eight essential questions:

1. Is your law practice focused exclusively on divorce and family law?

2. What attorney credentials do you bring to the representation?

3. Have you ever been sanctioned for an attorney ethics violation?

4. Will you be handling my divorce or will my case be handed off to another attorney with the firm?

5. How much will the legal representation cost?

6. Will I receive copies of every document in my case and will my calls be returned promptly?

7. How much experience do you have with complex high asset property divisions and finding hidden assets?

8. How much experience do you have with contested child custody matters?

This is a great opportunity to ask specific questions about your case and increase your knowledge about divorce. Don't be timid. Communicate any concerns you have regarding circumstances specific to your family situation. For example, if you have an older child with a disability, you might inquire about special needs child support and continued support for an adult-child. In your search, what you hope to find is a family law attorney who really listens to your concerns, who answers your questions, and who you can trust with the most important aspects of your personal life.

1. Is Your Law Practice Focused Exclusively on Divorce and Family Law?

There are three constants in family law — change, change, and change. Our courts continuously interpret and reinterpret the laws. Our legislatures stay busy passing new laws and amending existing ones. Our judges vary in how they apply the rules of court, rules of procedure, and rules of evidence in their courtrooms.

To navigate your way through this legal maze, you want a seasoned attorney nearby whose practice is focused exclusively on divorce and family law. By seasoned, I mean an attorney who has tried many divorce cases successfully. Someone who has worked with complex asset divisions and has handled contested custody matters. Someone who anticipates and strategizes with professional confidence built on years of experience. If you are interested in collaborative divorce, then ask if collaborative law is an area the attorney practices in. Not all do.

At Stewart Law Group, our family law attorneys exclusively practice divorce, paternity establishment, child custody, post-decree modifications, adoption, and related domestic relations matters. We have earned respect within the legal community for our outstanding trial skills, extensive knowledge of complex asset and property divisions, and diligent handling of child custody matters. Seek out the law firm and attorney in your community recognized for these same qualities and with a similarly stellar reputation.

2. What Attorney Credentials Do You Bring To the Representation?

Any attorney you consider hiring must be knowledgeable about Arizona's laws and the federal laws affecting your divorce. These include insurance laws, tax laws, domestic violence laws, child support laws, child custody laws, and so much more. Before you hire counsel, examine the profiles and credentials of the entire legal team at the law firm, from partners and associates to paralegals. A favorable outcome in your case may depend upon it!

For example, I am "AV Rated" by Martindale Hubbell and rated "Superb" by Avvo, Inc., with a 10-of-10 score. Both of these organizations consider peer reviews in rating attorneys, among other factors such as authorship and publications. Furthermore, every family lawyer with Stewart Law Group is dedicated to carry-ing out the law firm's mission and upholding the firm's reputation for excellence in the practice of divorce and family law. Everyone at my law firm is concerned with providing the best customer service possible. With a little online investigating into a firm's website and by simply asking the right questions, you can assure the law firm and attorney you ultimately choose will have the best credentials.

3. Have You Ever Been Sanctioned for an Attorney Ethics Violation?

Attorneys are held to high ethical standards with regard to the practice of law and the customer service they provide to their clients. You need assurance that the moral character and legal competency of your attorney justifies your hiring decision. The State Bar of Arizona regulates all of its attorney members and, when necessary, disciplines those lawyers with sanctions intended to punish for acts of professional misconduct. A grievance filed against an attorney may lead to reprimand, probation, suspension, restitution, and disbarment (the revocation of an attorney's license to practice law in the state).

At Stewart Law Group, practicing law with the utmost degree of ethics is at our firm's very core. We take great pride in our reputation for high professional ethical standards and successful, experienced, dedicated family law representation for our clients. None of our lawyers has been found in violation of an attorney ethics rule. If the attorney you interview or a member of that law firm has been disciplined by the state's bar association (or sanctioned in any other state), then you need to know about it before you decide to hire.

4. Will You Be Handling My Divorce or Will My Case Be Handed Off to Another Attorney With the Firm?

You may find that at some law firms the attorney who meets with you at the initial consultation is not the one who will be representing you in court. You deserve better than to have your case assigned to the lawyer with a light caseload that week! If you are interviewing one attorney but will be represented by another at the same law firm, then take the additional time to interview the attorney who will actually be handling your case. Yes, you have taken up some of the firm's time with the first interview. But really, is it asking too much to simply meet with your prospective advocate before you sign a retainer agreement and pay a retainer fee?

At Stewart Law Group, the attorney you meet at your initial interview, and with whom you enter into a signed representation agreement, will indeed be the attorney representing you throughout your divorce. Each of our attorneys develops a relationship of trust with their clients. A relationship that requires direct, open, and frequent communication between attorney and client. You should insist on meeting with the attorney who will actually represent and handle the divorce so you can assess whether the direct, open, and frequent communication necessary for a positive outcome is even possible.

5. How Much Will the Legal Representation Cost?

Cost is hugely important so do not shy away from asking this question. Ask, point blank, how much you will be charged for lawyer services and what the retainer fee will be, if any. Managing legal expenses requires planning and budgeting. To budget properly you need to know when you will be billed, so ask what the attorney's billing practices are. Some lawyers do not send statements out to their clients for months at a time. This could result in a surprisingly large bill covering months of services with an amount due that exceeds the funds you have available to pay.

Additionally, some attorneys charge a premium rate for their court appearances. Be sure to ask how the lawyer's *time* will be billed when working on your divorce. Some law firms charge a 15-minute minimum for any task, regardless of whether the work took the attorney five minutes or 15. If the attorney charges $300 an hour, for example, a five-minute telephone call could cost you $75!

By contrast, when meeting an attorney with Stewart Law Group, a thorough discussion on the cost of legal representation *always* precedes any signed representation agreement. We want every client to make an informed decision and be completely comfortable with our law firm's fee structure. To accomplish this, we carefully explain our billing system. When payments are due, the client is never surprised with hidden expenses or unexpected legal fees. We explain any costs and fees necessarily required in the client's divorce. We discuss our payment options as ways for the client to stay in control of his or her legal expenses. Our invoices are sent out once a month ensuring the client is aware of the work performed, how long the work took to complete, and what the cost was. Lastly, we do not charge higher rates for appearing in court on behalf of a client — our attorney rates always remain the same. These are precisely the up-front cost disclosures you need to know before your hire a divorce attorney.

6. Will I Receive Copies of Every Document in My Case and Will My Calls Be Returned Promptly?

When you interview a prospective attorney, be certain to ask how the law firm assures you will have access to all case documents whenever *you* need them. Nothing is more worrisome to clients than not knowing what has transpired in *their* divorce. Nothing is more frustrating for clients than being told to respond to pleadings they have never seen and know nothing about.

Unfortunately, some attorneys fail to provide their clients with copies of filed court documents (like motions from either party), orders issued by the court, or correspondences between the attorneys. To make matters worse, some lawyers chronically fail to return their client's telephone calls within a reasonable time. (That a client's call should be returned within 24 hours is a concept lost on some busy attorneys.)

So you know what to look for, at Stewart Law Group we make the best use of the most current technology to keep our clients fully engaged in their family law case. Substantive and procedural information on almost every topic in family law is readily available to clients on our website. Each can read-up on any subject relevant to the proceedings (or simply of interest to them) at any time, at no additional cost.

We also send the client copies of all divorce-related documents that either arrived at our office or left our office. If a client calls when the attorney or individual is not immediately available, then the call will be returned within 24 hours. That is the kind of outstanding customer service our clients highly value and something you should look for in your attorney.

Does the attorney and law firm have adequate internal management systems in place to assure that you are always apprised of what is happening in your divorce? Will you be able to reach your attorney when you need to, without unreasonable delay? If answers to these questions leave you doubting, then look elsewhere for competent legal representation and responsible customer service.

7. How Much Experience Do You Have with Complex High Asset Property Divisions and Finding Hidden Assets?

The division of assets and debts in some divorces may be very complex and openly contentious, which can be challenging for the parties, their attorneys, and the court. Adding strain to an already emotional situation, some individuals will attempt to conceal assets from the other spouse.

Not all divorce attorneys are knowledgeable about business valuations, stock portfolios, financing matters, tax and debt issues, or how to identify and successfully uncover hidden assets. Therefore, before you make the decision to hire a lawyer, you need to know whether that counselor is experienced in dealing with complex and high asset divorce cases. Does the attorney know how to search out clues to hidden assets?

If your spouse is suspected of deliberately concealing assets, then aggressive legal action must be taken by your lawyer to bring those assets before the court. You need an attorney and law firm that is vigilant, always on the lookout for clues in documents and lifestyle indicators of more money spent than the party claims to earn.

Whenever property division and debt settlement is complicated by a party's concealment, Stewart Law Group has the experience and financial tools necessary to ensure the client is not taken advantage of financially in the divorce. We routinely work with forensic accountants and investigators to uncover secreted assets and undeclared property. That diligent attention to detail and focus on the client's best interests is precisely what you should look for when interviewing an attorney prospect.

8. How Much Experience Do You Have with Contested Child Custody Matters?

Lastly, when you have minor children it is essential that your attorney be experienced with contested child custody matters, whether legal decision-making or parenting time is at issue. Not every divorce involves contested custody issues, but you want to hire the attorney who knows how to avoid problems without diminishing your legal position. You want the attorney who will not inflame (intentionally or unintentionally) an already highly emotional situation to the detriment of your children's best interests. You want an attorney who is prepared to advocate your position through litigation if you and your spouse cannot agree on custody.

In all child custody cases, whether part of a divorce or separately brought as a family law case, the dominant principal is awarding custody in accordance with the *best interests of the child*. In Arizona, there is no legal presumption favoring one parent over the other. If you desire sole legal decision-making or want the child living with you most of the time, then search for a legal advocate with lots of child custody experience.

At Stewart Law Group, we believe child custody is best settled through voluntary agreement between parents. We know from experience, however, that custody cases are often protracted and may need to be intensely litigated. In other words, voluntary settlement is not always possible. Consequently, your divorce attorney must be very knowledgeable of custody matters and be prepared to take legal action necessary to help you obtain the best custody arrangement possible.

Whenever custody is part of divorce, there are a number of procedures and professionals involved to assist in determining what is in the child's best interests. Mediation, parenting conferences, child custody evaluations, and settlement conferences are all part of custody determinations. The child may have legal advocates, too. A best interests attorney and child's attorney may be appointed to represent the minor throughout the court proceedings. Before committing to a particular firm, be sure to ask if the divorce attorney you are considering has ample experience with all of these custody procedures.

Working with Your New Divorce Attorney

Meeting with a lawyer for the first time is a very big step. When you commit to hiring a divorce attorney, the whole idea of terminating the marriage solidifies. Divorce is no longer a mere potentiality, it has become reality. That reality may seem overwhelmingly palpable for a while and strong emotions are to be expected, so don't be too tough on yourself. (Remember *Chapter 1* — when you need help dealing with the emotional aspects of your divorce, reach out and talk to a trusted friend, pastor, counselor, or family member.)

To help you through this transition, I'd like you to reflect on a few things as you begin working with your new divorce attorney.

First, be mindful that your attorney wants to help you move on with your life, the life that *you* imagine for yourself. Once you have explained your goals and objectives to your attorney, he or she knows what you need, want, and hope for. Your stated goals and objectives will influence your attorney at every step in the divorce process.

Second, bear in mind that your attorney is on your side, but there is no guarantee you will get everything you want and hope for. Keep your expectations realistic, while preparing to challenge the other party on those issues most important to you. Your attorney will explain each phase of the divorce so you understand what will be happening and how your rights and responsibilities will be affected. Whenever advocacy is needed, your attorney will be there to present your side within the confines of the family laws applicable to your divorce.

Third, be mindful that your attorney will be helping you through some very complicated issues, including the property settlement that is part and parcel of every divorce. Before you can even begin to negotiate a property settlement, your attorney will advise you on how property is divided. Once you understand your property rights and have classified assets and debts as either community property or separate property, you can start moving toward a property settlement.

Fourth, keep in mind that your attorney will be drafting any separation agreement you and your spouse have worked through. The agreement becomes enforceable for both of you by becoming part of the court's final decree of dissolution.

Fifth, know that throughout the entire family law case, your attorney will be scheduling and calendaring every significant date and deadline. This ensures every matter and every proceeding goes as smoothly as possible and that documents, pleadings, and hearings occur on time as scheduled without unnecessary delays. As each important date approaches, you will be given plenty of reminders of what you need to do and when you need to do it.

One final thought. This may be your first experience with divorce, but your lawyer has been through all of these procedures many times before. Rely on your attorney's advice and legal discernment. Rest assured knowing your legal advocate is working diligently on your behalf.

7

LIFE AFTER DIVORCE
Envision What Your New Life Will Be Like

This final chapter is all about you, your future, and the future you aspire to provide for your children. As is so often true in life, a good result begins with a good plan.

Standing at the courthouse steps with divorce papers in hand, recognize that you are not the same person you were when you married. Before traveling too far on the path to marital dissolution, reflect on what your life and lifestyle will be like after the divorce is finalized. You have grown and changed in many ways from the person who walked down the aisle so long ago. This is an opportunity to reinvent yourself. Only you know what dreams and aspirations are worth pursuing.

Moving on with a new life requires letting go of lingering hard feelings aimed at the other party. Hanging on to the baggage of angry thoughts and hurt feelings, blaming your spouse for what went wrong, will only sap your energy and waste your time. In my experience, the more blame and fault there is in a divorce, the more time it takes to resolve issues, the more the children will suffer, and the more money it costs the parties. Blame is toxic and will only hinder your ability to move forward with your goals and a new life. Do not let blame chain you to the past. Instead, keep your focus on the future and what you must do for yourself and for your children.

On the surface that sounds easy, but for some the idea of moving on alone can be overwhelming. If you are trapped in a painful emotional cycle and cannot break free from negative thoughts and feelings, then consider meeting with a divorce counselor. Together you can prepare for what lies ahead, step-by-step. In *Chapter 1*, I discussed the emotional issues often tied to divorce and stressed the importance of seeking help whenever you need it. You may want to review that chapter now.

Setting Goals for a Promising Future

You are committed to dissolving the marriage. But have you taken time to define important goals so you have some direction? Getting what you want from the divorce requires preparation and strategy. Where the parties are at after the divorce is final will depend, in part, on what happens during the divorce process. Once you know what it is you want, then you can begin setting realistic goals to achieve those ends.

Listing Long-Term and Short-Term Goals

There are many financial implications to divorce, all of which require thoughtful consideration. Start asking yourself key questions and write down your thoughts and answers. These will become the goals that guide you through the divorce and thereafter. Ask yourself:

- What will you need right away?
- How do you want to live?
- How will you support yourself?
- How will you support your children?
- Do you want career employment?
- Where do you want to live when the divorce is final?
- What will your lifestyle be like when you are on your own?
- What are your expectations for the distant future?
- When do you expect to retire?
- Will you send your children to college or university?

To stay on a path to *financial independence*, an employed spouse may plan for continuing education or the return to university for a degree. The spouse who has been unemployed for a lengthy period may plan on upgrading skills and seeking entry-level employment opportunities. A few questions to contemplate further:

- Will a job opportunity require relocation to another city or state?
- What is the cost of tuition and where will that money come from?
- Will spousal maintenance be needed? How much? For how long?
- Will student loans be necessary? If so, how much of a financial burden can you carry while working in the chosen field?
- Will an obligation to pay spousal support delay business pursuits or employment objectives?

Establishing long-term and short-terms goals is an important, necessary step in the divorce process. Take the task to heart and list your goals on paper. Leave yourself some breathing room to make changes later as needed.

Think of your long-term goals as the theme underscoring the vision you have for your future and your children's future. Short-term goals should keep you on track with accomplishing those long-term objectives.

For example, if your long-term goal is a career in physical therapy, then short-term goals may include finishing the degree program and preparing for certification.

With a clear vision for the future, implementing strategies to achieve your goals will become much easier during the divorce and thereafter. Before you take a position on any issue in your case, always reflect on the goals you set for yourself and stay focused on the outcome you desire.

Learn What the Law Requires of Both Parties

Successfully achieving the desired outcome in divorce depends largely upon the party's legal rights and obligations under Arizona law. Yes, you need to have clear goals, but you should also be realistic with those objectives. It would be unrealistic to ask the court for orders contrary to law, no judge has discretion to grant an unlawful request. Learn what is possible under the laws of this state and adjust your expectations to fit within those parameters.

Think about an example involving Arizona child custody law. How are legal decision-making and parenting time issues decided? One parent may seek substantially greater parenting time, asking the court to limit the other parent's schedule to "one weekend per month" during the school year. Given their circumstances, such a request may seem reasonable. Still, the judge has to apply all relevant statutory factors before making a final determination on a parenting time schedule. The court must consider the other spouse's legal right to parenting time. And even if the other parent agrees to such an arrangement, the court must still analyze each factor regarding the best interests of the child.

Freely Access Our Website as Your First Resource

I've been stressing the importance of getting a divorce education throughout this handbook, but you're probably wondering what's next. All of the legal information you need to get started in your divorce can be found at my firm's website.

For resources that build neatly and reliably on these chapters, visit *www.ArizonaLawGroup.com*. Always free, tap into our family law information hub whenever you have a question or want to confirm what you think you already know, just to be sure. Additional topics are there for you, including military divorce, prenuptial agreements, grandparents' rights, estate planning, and help for families in probate.

Read our blog, case summaries, key Arizona statutes and court rules. Find out who's who at Stewart Law Group (we have biographies for our attorneys and staff, all great people). Check out our other publications and ebooks. We even compiled a list of recommended authors who have written about divorce and family law matters, some for adult readers, some for kids.

When you're on the website, sign up for our free *e-Divorce Course*. If you have children, then sign up for our free *e-Custody Course* as well. Don't worry, it's self-paced with no tests. (I promise!) These email courses will walk you through each court proceeding, linking you to specific discussions, statutes, and focus articles on our website. These courses are great companions to the Arizona Divorce Handbook.

When you envision your future and begin setting goals, do so with a firm understanding of what is legally possible under Arizona law. As you prepare for life after divorce, start thinking about making necessary changes to your insurance coverage and estate plan, too.

Changing Insurance Coverage

Getting a grip on finances after divorce also requires careful examination of your insurance coverage. Whenever circumstances change significantly, as with a divorce, any insured person should review certificates of insurance for automobile, homeowner's, life, and disability insurance coverage. Update insurers with your new contact information. If the other party is ordered to pay the premiums and a payment is missed, for any reason, then you need to be notified immediately. Be sure to speak with an insurance agent about the risks and benefits associated with any changes to premiums, deductibles, or basic policy coverage before committing to those changes.

Minimum Automobile Insurance Coverage

Your insurance budget will have to cover a number of policies, including mandatory insurance for your personal vehicle. Premiums depend upon the make, model, year, and condition of the vehicle, the distances regularly driven, driving record, and credit history. Under the *Fair Credit Reporting Act (FCRA)*,[1] insurance companies have a "permissible purpose" in examining a potential insured's credit information. When problems leading up to divorce involved financial issues between the spouses or bankruptcy, then negative credit information and a low credit score could result in higher premiums.

In Arizona, a *certificate of insurance* is necessary to register a vehicle and drive lawfully. The minimum automobile insurance coverage to operate a vehicle legally is bodily injury liability coverage ($15,000 per person, $30,000 per accident) and property damage liability coverage ($10,000 per accident).

For coverage beyond the required minimum, expect premiums to increase correspondingly. *Bodily injury coverage* pays for injuries the insured caused to others in an accident, but it does not pay for the insured's injuries (for that, add *medical payments coverage* to the policy). *Property damage* coverage pays for the damage the insured caused to other vehicles or property in an accident, but it does not pay for damage to the insured's vehicle (for that, add *collision coverage* to the policy).

For the insurance company to pay for damage or loss to the insured's vehicle because of theft, glass breakage, fire, violent weather, vandalism, hitting an animal, and so on, add *comprehensive coverage* to the policy. Talk to your insurance agent. Carefully go over each option and the cost associated with it.

Selecting Homeowner's Insurance

If there is a mortgage or deed of trust on your home, then you must have sufficient *property damage coverage* to satisfy the lender's minimum insurance requirements. Should your home be totally destroyed, as the borrower you are still obligated to pay off the loan. Make certain the homeowner's insurance policy sufficiently covers the debt should a destructive event occur, such as a fire.

Property damage coverage includes loss to the real property. *Contents insurance* covers loss of personal property and possessions located at or inside the home. When the homeowner has special collections, expensive jewelry, valuable antiques, or sophisticated computer equipment, for instance, additional contents coverage should be scheduled to ensure adequate protection against the loss of these valuable items.

Personal liability insurance coverage protects the insured should someone be injured on the property as a result of homeowner negligence or for which the homeowner becomes legally responsible. The insurance company covers the defense costs up to the agreed upon limit stated in the policy.

If anyone tends to landscaping or makes repairs to the home, then there is a risk the worker could be injured with the homeowner potentially held liable for damages. With *medical payments insurance* coverage, someone injured on the premises will have some or all medical expenses paid without regard to fault for the injury. This coverage does not extend to any intentional acts of the homeowner, however, and does not cover a renter, home business, the homeowner or a family member residing there.

When comparing insurance premiums, be prepared to answer questions about your home's construction, the year it was built, the location of fire hydrants, the distance to the nearest fire station, among other details. In Arizona's outlying areas, the nearest fire station may be miles away resulting in higher premiums for rural homeowners.

What to Do About Life Insurance?

A life insurance policy pays out a specific amount of money to the beneficiary in the event of the insured's death. During the marriage, couples often have life insurance policies that name the "surviving spouse" as the primary beneficiary. Once the divorce is final, an immediate change in beneficiary designation may be in order. Most insurers require the use of their official change of beneficiary designation form, mailed to the policyholder upon request.

As part of the divorce settlement, the party ordered to pay child support or spousal maintenance may also be required to maintain a life insurance policy to ensure those support payments continue after the death of the obligor. If you are the one receiving support, you may have concerns about the policy lapsing or the beneficiary being changed without your knowledge. If you have those concerns and want to stay in control of the situation, then you could arrange to pay the premiums on the life insurance policy yourself.

Term life insurance policies provide coverage for a specific length of time. They have no equity or cash value, so a term life policy is not an investment tool. As the insured gets older, either the premium increases or the pay-out on death decreases. When it comes to cost savings, term life policies are useful alternatives and easiest on the budget.

A *variable life insurance* policy is a combination of insurance and investment. Investments always involve some level of risk. Once the money is taken out to pay the insurance premium, the remainder is invested. For this policy to work as an investment vehicle, more money is paid by the policyholder than is needed to cover the insurance premiums. There is a guaranteed minimum payment upon death under the insurance. There is a potential the invested portion will also provide money upon death. As with any investment, there is no guaranteed rate of return. These policies tend to be much more costly than other life insurance products.

The *whole life insurance* policy provides coverage over the course of the insured's lifetime at a set premium. Typically, the premium is paid over the duration of the policy, right up until the death of the insured. Unless the policyholder is willing to pay life insurance premiums for life, other insurance products may be more useful and cost effective.

Why Disability Insurance Coverage?

Individual *disability insurance* will cover an insured's monthly income for a specific period if rendered unable to work because of illness or injury. For the party paying spousal maintenance or child support, a disability insurance policy can cover expenses if he or she becomes disabled and cannot earn an income. Many people fall into arrears on their support obligations because of accidents and sickness. Even a few months of disability coverage could make a big difference with support compliance.

What About COBRA?

If one spouse is covered by the other spouse's employer insurance program, then the divorce is a "qualifying event" that gives the non-employee spouse COBRA coverage for up to three years (or 36 months). COBRA may represent a cost-savings compared to independently acquired coverage. Still, the premiums must be paid or coverage will lapse.

With every insurance decision, carefully reflect on your comfort level of risk given the insurance budget you have to work with. Do the most you can with the resources you have available after the divorce. When discussing coverage with an insurance agent, get all of your questions answered before agreeing to take on a new policy or deciding to change or terminate an existing policy.

Revising Estate Plans After Divorce

Soon you will begin a fresh and independent chapter in your life with new objectives and responsibilities. Because your legal status and financial circumstances are about to undergo a major transformation, take an evening or Saturday afternoon to carefully review your estate plan. The following instruments are typically found in estate plans:

Checklist

✓ *Last Will and Testament*

✓ *Letter of Instruction for Funeral and Burial*

✓ *Beneficiary Deed*

✓ *Durable General Power of Attorney*

✓ *Limited Power of Attorney*

✓ *Health Care Power of Attorney*

✓ *HIPPA Authorization*

✓ *Living Trust or Inter Vivos Trust*

✓ *Payable-on-Death Accounts (POD Accounts)*

✓ *Life Insurance Policy*

Isolate those of your estate planning documents needing modification or revocation (termination). If you do not have an estate plan yet, then this is an excellent opportunity to start conceptualizing one. You may wish to schedule a consultation with an estate planning attorney while the divorce is still pending. Although you can certainly *prepare* to revise your estate plan during the divorce, refrain from taking any action that might violate the preliminary injunction. (Visit my firm's website for estate planning and probate representation and information.)

The most basic component of an estate plan is the *Last Will and Testament.* We should all periodically re-examine our Last Wills to ensure that they are consistent with our current testamentary intentions. Reviewing your estate plan every three to five years is good practice as a general rule. Additionally, you should review your estate plan whenever life circumstances significantly change. In addition to divorce and annulment, examples of life-changing events are the birth of one's first child, a substantial inheritance from a wealthy relative, and winning the lottery.

Consider what could happen if you were to die without a Last Will before finalization of your divorce. All of assets could go to your "surviving spouse" under Arizona intestate succession law.[2] Death of a spouse terminates the divorce proceedings and the other party, as surviving spouse, would be heir at law.

One or the Other, Testate or Intestate

When a person died with a Last Will and Testament, he or she is said to have died *testate*. The enforceable terms of the Last Will control administration of the decedent's testate estate, appointment of an executor, and distribution to the devisees named therein.

By contrast, a person who died without a Last Will is said to have died *intestate*. Arizona's intestate succession law applies to administration of the decedent's intestate estate, appointment of a personal representative, and controls distribution of assets to the heirs at law. With intestate succession, Arizona statutory law determines who the heirs are. The statute determines who will inherit from you when you are deceased, and who will not. The only way to change that outcome is to have an estate plan with a Last Will or trust that serves a testamentary function.

This is important. If your Last Will was drafted during the marriage, then your spouse was probably named executor (or personal representative) of your estate as well as your primary devisee (or beneficiary). You may have left *everything* to your spouse upon your death! Be sure to review your estate documents early on, while the divorce is pending.

One important caveat. Although some changes could be made to your estate plan without violating the preliminary injunction in the divorce (for example, a change in healthcare power of attorney and living will), you can have a completely revised estate plan prepared and ready for your signature as soon as the divorce decree is entered.

There is one more thing I want to talk to you about. Saving money in your divorce.

How to Reduce the Cost of Your Divorce

Of course, every divorce involves unique circumstances and complexities. In my experience, there is one commonality — the need to keep attorney fees and legal expenses under control. As a wrap-up to this chapter, here are six money-saving tips to help you keep the costs associated with your divorce at a minimum.

Tip #1: Start Your Divorce Education Today

You know how important I think it is that you educate yourself on the family law issues relevant to your case. (Your decision to pick up this handbook was a great place to begin!) Just as with any new job, once you have a reasonable understanding of the task at hand your efficiency will improve markedly. That includes an improved capacity to focus negotiations with your spouse and strategic discussions with your attorney.

You are not preparing for paralegal certification, yet you do need to understand routine domestic relations issues. If you have children, then learn what is involved in developing a parenting plan and establishing child support. If you are a small business owner, then learn how the division of community assets and debts will affect your company's future. If you are a service member, then learn how military pensions are divided in divorce.

Consider setting aside one hour each day to study the general concepts of divorce — parenting time, legal decision-making authority, child support, spousal maintenance, and property division. Familiarize yourself with the legal terminology and court procedures. By doing so, you will grasp the issues and strategies in your case more quickly, with less explanation time needed from your lawyer. By raising the bar, you will extract more from consultations and be better positioned to engage your attorney on the finer points and legal nuances in your case. The more knowledgeable you are about issues in your divorce, the more informed your decisions will be.

Tip #2. Avoid Litigation to Resolve Disputed Issues

Litigation is a very expensive method for resolving disputed issues in a divorce. If you really hope to save money, then avoid litigation at every opportunity. And never attempt to use litigation as a way of punishing your spouse.

I talked about alternatives to litigation in *Chapter 2*. Whenever appropriate, utilizing ADR methods can help resolve numerous issues, if not all disputed matters. Once the list of contested issues is winnowed down to what simply cannot be resolved through negotiation, mediation, or other ADR proceedings, then remaining matters are litigated at trial. Less issues litigated at trial, less money spent on attorney's fees and court costs.

Tip #3. When You Have Agreement, Write It Down

When you and your spouse come to an agreement on any issue, write it down. Agreed on who takes the vehicle? Write it down. Agreed on who stays in the marital home? Write it down. Every agreement represents one less issue to be resolved through negotiation, mediation, or litigation. You may actually find you are in mutual agreement on a number of major decisions that must be made.

Tip #4. Hire an Attorney With a Reasonable Fee Arrangement

Just as a reminder, when choosing an attorney look for a lawyer who tells you upfront what the fees will be. Attorneys are not clairvoyant, but they should anticipate the proceedings and how many attorney hours are likely to be involved at each step. The attorney's billable rate must be discussed at the initial consultation. To allow budgeting, you need to know how often the attorney bills, how much of a retainer fee is required, and whether different services have different rates.

What you definitely do not need is an attorney who routinely delays the case and drags the divorce process out. That approach will cost you more money while adding to your stress level. You deserve nothing less than efficiency and proficiency from your divorce attorney.

Tip #5. Apply Cost-Benefit Analysis to Every Issue

The adage "choose your battles wisely" has application in divorce. Not every issue is worth fighting over. Be selective. What concerns you most? Be practical by spending your divorce dollars on the issues you've targeted, as much as circumstances allow. Although it can be challenging at times, do not allow emotions to interfere with rational thinking.

When you look at every issue from a cost-benefit perspective, you cannot help but stay focused on getting the divorce finished and done with. If you had to choose, would you prefer to pay your attorney to negotiate a used-microwave oven or spousal maintenance? Which is more important? This example may seem silly, but people do get caught up in their emotions and what they perceive to be a fairness issue. When it comes to negotiations, focus on the important issues and let little things go by the wayside.

Tip #6. Do Much of the Basic Leg-Work Yourself

The time and effort you put into being fully prepared will save you money. When your attorney asks for photocopies of all financial accounts, be thorough and provide complete copies. You want your attorney to be businesslike and efficient, you should be the same. Maximize your attorney's time, do not waste it. For example, you do not need to speak to your attorney directly (and pay the attorney hourly rate) when the legal assistant has that information for you.

No matter who among your legal team is on the telephone with you, keep your conversations brief and to the point. When you have a conference scheduled with your attorney, be fully prepared for the issues to be discussed. When in negotiations, consistently take reasonable positions even when the other party does not. Always be mindful of the need to steer clear of litigation whenever possible. Remember, "time is money." And it's the attorney's time and your money that we're talking about.

By taking a practical approach to cost reduction at each stage in the divorce, you will enjoy significant savings over the entire process. A divorce can be quite economical, especially when the parties are cooperative with each other.

Chapter Notes

1. 15 USC § 1681 et seq.

2. ARS § 14-2102. Intestate share of surviving spouse.

Scott David Stewart, Esq.

Born and raised in Phoenix, author Scott David Stewart is the founding attorney of Stewart Law Group. His vision was to establish a unique law firm singularly focused on the clients' experiences when dealing with difficult and often intensely emotional legal matters.

With eight office locations throughout the Valley of the Sun, today this influential law firm represents clients in all matters of divorce, child custody and family law, accident and personal injury, estate planning and probate, professional license defense, DUI defense, and general criminal defense.

Early in his professional career, Scott Stewart was Deputy County Attorney in the Major Crimes Division of the Maricopa County Attorney's Office. As a felony prosecutor, Stewart honed his trial skills and developed the strategies for success that he continues to implement today in all aspects of his law practice. Since its formation, Stewart Law Group has earned the trust and respect of clients from all walks of life.

Scott Stewart is a member of the State Bar of Arizona, Maricopa County Bar Association, and American Bar Association. He has an AV Preeminent® attorney-rating from Martindale-Hubbell® and is also rated "Superb" by Avvo, Inc. Stewart Law Group is an accredited Arizona business with the Better Business Bureau having received an A+ rating.

With more than seven decades of combined legal experience, Scott Stewart and Stewart Law Group take on the most complex and challenging cases. To read more about the author, his recognitions, awards, and client testimonials, visit www.ArizonaLawGroup.com.

Other Books
By
SCOTT DAVID STEWART

Tactical Guide to Prenuptial Agreements in Arizona

Arizona Child Custody Essentials,
What Every Parent Needs to Know

The Arizona DUI Handbook

Subpoena Compliance, Appearance, Objection, and Protective
Orders in Arizona Mental Health Practice

Stewart Law Group

777 E Thomas Rd Ste 210, Phoenix AZ 85014
Phone: 602.548.4600

Phoenix • Scottsdale • Chandler
Glendale • Mesa • Peoria
Tempe • Gilbert

www.ArizonaLawGroup.com

Made in the USA
Columbia, SC
27 August 2022

65975980R00109